THE Rescued DOG
Problem Solver

TRACY LIBBY

i-5
PRESS

The Rescued Dog Problem Solver

Project Team
Editor: Heather Russell-Revesz
Copy Editor: Joann Woy
Design: Mary Ann Kahn
Index: Elizabeth Walker

i-5 PUBLISHING, LLC™
Chief Executive Officer: Mark Harris
Chief Financial Officer: Nicole Fabian
Chief Content Officer: June Kikuchi
Chief Digital Officer: Jennifer Black
Chief Marketing Officer: Beth Freeman Reynolds
General Manager, i-5 Press: Christopher Reggio
Art Director, i-5 Press: Mary Ann Kahn
Senior Editor, i-5 Press: Amy Deputato
Production Director: Laurie Panaggio
Production Manager: Jessica Jaensch

Library of Congress Cataloging-in-Publication Data
ISBN: 978-1-62008-139-6 has been applied for.

This book has been published with the intent to provide accurate and authoritative information in regard to the subject matter within. While every precaution has been taken in the preparation of this book, the author and publisher expressly disclaim any responsibility for any errors, omissions, or adverse effects arising from the use or application of the information contained herein. The techniques and suggestions are used at the reader's discretion and are not to be considered a substitute for veterinary care. If you suspect a medical problem, consult your veterinarian.

i-5 Publishing, LLC™
3 Burroughs, Irvine, CA 92618
www.facebook.com/i5press
www.i5publishing.com

Printed and bound in China
15 16 17 18   1 3 5 7 9 8 6 4 2

Contents

Foreword

On December 14, 2011, my parents and I stopped at a local shelter and rescued J'mee—a scruffy white Terrier mix. She is not my family's first rescue dog, nor will she be our last. Yet, she got me thinking, "What if?" Could I connect the world of rescue using images and stories of success to drive change in the public's perception of rescue dogs? Watching J'mee change from a worried, confused little gal into a confident, wonderfully silly, loving companion was the catalyst, the inspiration that turned stories and images into messages of hope.

I have tried to capture the unique life and personality within each dog, the soul inside the endless contrasts of breed, size, personality, scars, scruffy coats, and experiences these dogs have encountered over the years that they have been loved, lost, abandoned, abused, surrendered, or, in some cases, forgotten.

I have tried, as much as possible, to pare away the more shocking details and instead focus on unleashing the true essence of each dog, as well as their typical and sometimes unique training challenges. Each of these dogs is incredible in his or her own way, as are their owners. I'm so thankful to have had the lucky privilege to meet them, to spend time with them, and to have the opportunity to share their ridiculously cute, quirky personalities and stories of success. They make my heart sing, make me giggle, and make me cry happy tears for having been lucky enough to meet them.

Hats off and a million thanks to the owners who shared their dogs' stories so I could bring them to all of you.

I dedicate this book to the shelter dogs who waited patiently for their permanent homes, and to those who continue to wait. To the dogs who make our lives worth living. The dogs who hunt, herd, retrieve, catch Frisbees, chase balls, and swim. To the dogs who warm our hearts, make us grin from ear to ear, remind us of the beauty of love, and fill our lives with purpose and passion.

Introduction

The fact that you're reading this book probably means that you have adopted—or intend to adopt—a shelter/rescue dog. That, in turn, means your life is about to change for the better!

Dogs demand a lot of attention—some more so than others, depending on their breed, history, temperament, and personality. Yet dogs pay us back with an endless range of benefits. The obvious perks include companionship and lower blood pressure, but what about the silliness that is so contagious it practically oozes out of some dogs' fur? Do you ever want to break out in a happy dance at your dog's pure happiness? Maybe gazing at his goofy, lovable face makes you grin uncontrollably from ear to ear? What about the wiggly dog who cheers up even the crummiest of days? And don't forget the dog who makes you cry happy tears for being nothing short of perfect. These magic moments are what make loving dogs super special. Unbreakable bonds between dogs and owners are created in these moments, and they make being in the company of dogs a blessing.

Although dogs are incredible creatures, giving you the impression that it's all clear sailing ahead would be disingenuous. Sure, your dog will make you laugh harder than you ever imagined, but he may also potty on your best carpet, commit heinous crimes against your personal property, refuse to come when called, and embarrass you in front of your in-laws. (If you were looking to avoid public humiliation, you should have considered a cat!)

My primary motive for writing this book is to share with you the amazing journey of twelve shelter dogs who were facing uncertain futures. Yet through the love and dedication of their equally remarkable owners, as well as plenty of committed volunteers who saw past their often sad, sunken exterior, these dogs are now living a life of endless kisses, cuddles, and love. Some, like Lily Bella, Queso, and Casey, have gone on to be perfect hiking, jogging, camping, or horse backing riding companions. Others, like Kota and Levi have excelled in canine sports. All of them were at one time discarded, lost, or abandoned, yet they have become treasured companions in the eyes of their owners.

So what will you find in this book? In addition to the personal journey of these twelve remarkable rescue dogs, you will find lots of material that will help you to build a mutually respectful and loving human-canine relationship (because everything about dog training comes down to the relationship you have with your dog). You will learn about the "transition period"—that period of time, which can be a few days, weeks, or months—when your dog may be nervous, anxious, fearful, and really not himself as he adjusts to his new home. You'll learn the benefits of interactive play and how to use it to build confidence and enthusiasm and instill desired behaviors or to physically and mentally burn excess energy and tire out a high-energy dog. You will also learn how to teach basic obedience commands and fun tricks, as well as to problem solve solutions.

I hope you will also learn to look at your own emotions and traits to determine your behavior, which has a huge impact on your dog's behavior. If, for example, you are harsh and overbearing, unsympathetic, insecure, impatient, arrogant, pessimistic, and so forth, you will have a profoundly negative effect on your dog. If, on the other hand, you are funny, silly, animated, invigorating, upbeat, kind, patient, and so forth, you will have a positive effect on your dog.

Finally, plenty of wonderful methods for training dogs exist, and I have endeavored to share many of them with you. Throughout the book, I have reinforced the use of positive reinforcement. Granted, positive reinforcement doesn't necessarily mean being nice, it simply means adding something that your dog finds reinforcing, such as cookie or toy, and, although other options exist, I think you will find positive reinforcement serves you well in most instances.

Whether you start with a puppy, junior, or adult dog, the same principles of training apply because behaviors are shaped by repetition and by building each lesson on the previous one, step-by-step. The length of time a dog can train or the rate at which he learns will vary depending on his age, temperament, energy level, history, owner involvement, and so forth. Consider, for example, that a training session for an eight- or ten-week-old puppy may be two or three minutes several times a day. Yet, a five- or six- month-old dog can usually work for ten or fifteen minutes several times a day, whereas a high-drive, high-energy dog will most certainly need more than a ten-minute stroll around the block!

My hope is that this book will inspire and help you to build a zany, happy, mutually loving and respectful human-canine relationship. Most of all, I hope to make training fun for both you and your dog. After all, if there's no joy in it, what's the point?

As you read, no doubt you will come across some ideas that you love and others that seem questionable or downright nutty. You may find that some tools, techniques, and solutions will work for you and that some will work better for others. That's okay. As you build your own mosaic of knowledge, your job as a responsible dog owner will be to sort through the myriad training techniques and pick those that work successfully for you and your dog. It is my hope that, by the end of the book, you have lots of options to choose from and you can tailor your training methods to fit your dog's specific needs.

Chapter 1

Safe Introductions

J'MEE AND JAKE— A TALE OF TWO TERRIERS

Scruffy white terrier mix J'mee was an owner release—surrendered to a California animal shelter in 2011 because she was "too energetic" and "bullied" the family's older dog. An all too familiar story of a first-rate dog surrendered and destined for an uncertain future through no fault of her own. With an abundance of tears, the owner relinquished J'mee, left abruptly, and never looked back.

All smiles and exuding uncontrollable glee, Jake, an intact terrier mix, was picked up roaming the streets of Perris, California, in 2014. How long the one-year-old dog had been on the streets is anyone's guess. If he once had a home, he had been gone a long time. His ratty, matted coat, and skin-and-bones physique suggested a scavenger's life. Jake had no collar, no tags, no microchip, no ID. Zip. Zero. Nada.

Adopting a shelter or rescue dog can seem like a roll of the dice. Rescuing a terrier (or two!) can add additional elements of risk simply because of the breed's wide range of characteristics, which run with individual variations throughout the terrier clans thirty recognized breeds. Generally speaking, terriers tend to like people, but many have little tolerance for other animals, including other dogs—and especially other terriers.

Bred to "go to ground," hunting vermin is a vocation and a passion for many terriers, one that has been passed down through the generations. Characteristically feisty, terriers enjoy a good scrap but a willingness to fight is different than a bad temperament. Rescuing

RESCUED DOG J'MEE IS AN ADORABLE SCRUFFY WHITE TERRIER MIX.

a terrier or terrier mix requires a savvy owner who understands these pint-sized, full-of-spunk dogs. My parents, despite my cautious advice, knew J'mee was perfect. They shelled out the adoption fee and sprung from the shelter the unbelievably cute two-year-old mix.

A recipe for disaster? One might assume so. After all, high-energy dogs are not the best match for senior citizens (even very active senior citizens), and terriers can be the quintessential high-energy

JAKE, RESCUED BY THE SAME COUPLE WHO RESCUED J'MEE, IS AN AFFECTIONATE, HAPPY TERRIER MIX.

dogs. Overall, my parents lucked out. J'mee bonded almost instantly to my parents, but she remained a bit worried and uncertain for the first weeks. Her sensory system appeared overwhelmed by new owners, a new home, and new sights and smells. Car rides remained traumatic and were accompanied by uncontrollable shaking and trembling. Possibly she was experiencing flashbacks from the car ride that betrayed her trust and left her abandoned? She knew Sit and Down, and she was housetrained, crate trained, and lap trained. But she did have a few naughty habits. This frisky girl may never have gone to ground like her ancestors, but she has the terrier's characteristic quick spirit. She notices all comings and goings of people, cats, and dogs. She fancies sitting at the window watching for passersby—preferably ones walking a dog—at which time she screams through the doggie door at 70 mph (112 kph), racing from one side of the house to the other squealing and barking until she chases away the "trespassers." Once mission accomplished status has been satisfied, she resumes her position at the window to restart the "game."

More problematic, she is an escape artist. She cannot be trusted off leash in any unsecured environment. She will take off if she gets loose and will keep on running until she is long gone out of Dodge. A gates-closed-at-all-times policy, coupled with patience, positive training, and consistent reinforcement have allowed her to make progress; however, not yet

THANKS TO CAREFUL INTRODUCTIONS, JAKE AND J'MEE ARE NOW INSEPARABLE COMPANIONS.

and possibly never to the point of being off leash in an unsecured environment.

Two years after rescuing J'mee, my now 84-year-old parents rescued Jake. Despite his renegade street-dog existence, the one-year-old terrier mix is a charmer. The happiest of happy dogs, Jake is an affectionate extrovert, inquisitive, and adventurous with a big and enjoyable spirit. His pedigree is unknown, but in keeping with the terrier's classic characteristics, he is energetic with a delightful sense of humor but more mischievous than feisty. Half terrier. Half backhoe. Jake loves to dig, dig, and dig some more. A highly prized manicured lawn now resembles a land mine of brown patches and potholes. Yet, Jakey, as he's affectionately called, stole the hearts of everyone, especially his canine sibling J'mee. The two terriers are thick as thieves. Head over heels. And holy smokes, how they love to run! Watching the two of them posture, then suddenly take off zooming across the yard, darting around trees and under bushes makes you laugh so hard tears stream down your face.

Of course, it was not quite love at first sight. J'mee needed to show Jakey the ropes, and it took a few days of jockeying and posturing and a few snarky moments for the two dogs to establish the ground rules and be comfortable living together. Today, they are inseparable—eating, playing, and sleeping together. Jake is simply the perfect canine companion for J'mee, and vice versa. The situation easily could have been disastrous, but sometimes life has a way of delivering the right dogs at the right time to the right people.

Introducing a New Canine Family Member

Ideally, adding a second (or third!) dog to the family should be well planned out, with a good deal of thought directed toward a compatible canine buddy to your existing dog. Should you get a puppy or adult dog? Small or large dog? Male or female? Energetic or low-key personality? Do you really want another dog just for the sake of having another dog? Some owners get another dog as a companion for their existing dog. That's all well and good, and for Jake and J'mee the situation worked out well. Unfortunately, there is no way of guaranteeing in advance if that will be the case. Not every dog will want to live with other dogs.

Then there are those times when life doesn't work out as planned. Sure, you never intended to get another dog, but one day you find yourself driving home with an adorable furry addition in the backseat and thinking, "Now what?"

Prevention: Creating a Safe Environment

Adding a new dog to your current environment can double your fun and companionship. In the long run, things will probably work out fine, but in the beginning, it is wise to take a few precautionary steps to make all dogs feel good about the situation. Creating an environment that is safe and comfortable for all dogs involved and promotes a positive, tension-free friendship will go a long way in helping to ensure a successful transition. After all, the main goal of introductions is for it to be a positive experience for all dogs involved.

Did You Know? THE MORE THE MERRIER!

If you are adding a second or third dog to your existing canine family, you are in good company. According to the American Veterinary Medical Association's 2012 U.S. Pet Ownership and Demographics Source book, as of 2011:

- An estimated 74.1 million dogs live in the United States in nearly 44 million homes, which equates to roughly 36.5 percent of the population.
- Six out of ten households own one dog.
- 26 percent of households own two dogs.
- 7.5 percent own three dogs.
- Slightly less than 5 percent (4.7 percent) own four or more dogs.

Equally interesting, 29 percent of pet owners said they would add a mixed breed as their next dog, with shelters (44.9 percent) and rescue organizations (39.8 percent) being mentioned most often as sources to be used if acquiring a dog.

Understanding your rescue's temperament and breed tendencies can help make introductions smoother.

Some dogs are naturally calm and get along beautifully with other dogs from the get-go. In these instances, introductions may go off without a hitch, and all your dogs will be fast friends. This happens quite often, but plenty of trainers and behaviorists will cite cases in which introductions were rushed, forced, or unsupervised, and the dogs ended up despising each other from then on. Some owners, as well as a few trainers, opt for the free-for-all method, where they toss the new dog in with all the other dogs and let them sort it out. While this may work in rare instances, it is not recommended. Some dogs are more territorial than others, and you run the risk of causing lifelong relationship issues between the dogs—not to mention an increased likelihood of physical and emotional harm.

To be comfortable, your new puppy or adult dog needs to know he is safe and that the other dog (or dogs) won't bully, intimidate, or hurt him. The same goes for your existing dog. He needs to know he can trust the newest family member.

Introducing Other Dogs

Luckily, dogs are social animals, and when well-socialized as youngsters they tend to grow into adult dogs who enjoy the company of other dogs. Sadly, some dogs develop unwanted behaviors while living with their previous owners. Others become stressed, anxious, or fearful while living on the streets or confined to a shelter situation.

No one single plan for dog-to-dog introductions exist. General guidelines will help to increase the odds of a smooth and minimally stressful transition. Yet much will depend on the temperament, personality, and size of the dogs; to some extent, each dog's breed; and whether the new dog you are adding is a puppy, junior, or adult dog. Are any of the dogs anxious, fearful, sight or sound sensitive, dominant, or dog-to-dog aggressive? What are their play styles and energy levels? Equally important, what are the established preferences of your existing dog? Understanding each dog's breed history, if you know it, will help you determine his or her individual traits. For example, J'mee, while her pedigree is unknown, appears to be part West Highland Terrier—a breed that can be cocky and tough and "Scottish to the core." If your dog is part Boxer, it's a good idea to understand that they play by standing on their hind legs and "boxing," which can be intimidating and off putting to many dogs. Or, if you've rescued a high-drive, high-energy herding dog, you'll need to understand that they like to control movement, which often includes nipping.

For multiple-dog households, consider introducing your new dog, be it a puppy or adult, to one dog at a time. If you know both dogs are social and friendly with other dogs, the introduction should be easy. Most humane societies and rescue organizations do temper and personality evaluations before releasing dogs for adoption. That said, not all shelter staff are knowledgeable about canine body language, and dogs living in a shelter environment can quickly deteriorate emotionally and therefore may not be accurately evaluated.

Meeting Outdoors

Ideally, introductions should be made outside in a quiet, open area and, if possible, on neutral territory, such as during a short walk together around the block or a friend's yard. This gives the dogs plenty of room to negotiate, and they are not forced to interact in a small space. This is doubly important if you are uncertain how the dogs will react. A nearby park may work but be careful of too much stimulation, such as other dogs or loud, rambunctious kids. Consider enlisting the help of a friend, family member, or experienced dog trainer who can handle one of the dogs.

Ideally, introductions should be made on neutral territory, such as a short walk together around the block.

Depending on each dog's temperament, personality, and individual characteristics, a fenced yard, field, or tennis court, works well—provided it is a safe environment. For example, two socially friendly dogs, with little or no emotional baggage or aggressive tendencies, may quickly accept each other on their own terms if allowed to interact unencumbered in a fenced-in area without owner interference. No pressure on either of the dogs. While some experts caution against this type of introduction, many an owner has inadvertently created a good deal of canine anxiety by attempting to force interactions between the dogs or jerking or tightening the tension on the leash, which can escalate to canine threats or aggression.

If going off leash is not possible, consider letting the dogs drag their leashes on the ground. If that isn't possible, use a 6-foot (100 cm) leash or long line but be sure to keep the leash or long line loose at all times.

While there are numerous advantages to introducing dogs on neutral territory, sometimes it isn't possible. In these instances, your yard is better than inside the house. Urinating and marking are normal ways dogs meet, greet, and find out anything and everything about each other, and outdoor meetings allow them this opportunity. Inside your home can create additional stress because of the inability to "mark"—or they may mark your couch, which does not get things off to a good start! Plus, indoors may not provide the open space dogs need to adequately check each other out. Some dogs are more territorial than others, and being indoors, which forces dogs to investigate each other at close range, may create additional problems.

With any dog-to-dog interactions, you must be observant. Brush up on your canine body language skills so you can recognize when either dog is worried, anxious, fearful, or simply being a bully. Also, keep things moving. It's probably one of the most important things you

Training Tip: TRANSITION PERIOD

Right away, you knew he was the dog for you! Yet, most likely, your dog doesn't know what is happening, especially if he was an owner release to an animal shelter. His world has been turned upside down. He may see you as the latest person to shake up his life, including his sense of stability and security (if he ever had any!). A new environment, sights, smells, and sounds can be overwhelming. He may not understand that he gets to stay with you forever, and that you've got his back no matter what. Subsequently, stressing or acting out is not uncommon for many dogs. Take your time, provide him with plenty of guidance and direction and love, and allow him to adjust at his own pace.

can do to help dogs become comfortable with each other. For example, if one or all of the dogs get up on their hackles, stare at each other, or the like—tell them in a happy, calm voice, "Hey, guys, let's go this way"—or whatever is necessary to calmly break up the potentially tense get-together. If you start walking in a purposeful way, the dogs, or at least one of them, should follow. The key is to move away from the dogs, which helps to diffuse additional tension. This is a difficult concept for many owners because human nature is to move toward the dogs.

Next Steps

Once the dogs have completed the "meet and greet" outside and appear comfortable with each other, then you can move them indoors. However, until you are certain how they will react, do not leave them alone. Again, baby gates and ex-pens are great for separating dogs yet still allowing

It's important to make introductions positive and stress-free.

them to see each other. This also prevents them from being forced to interact, and gives them plenty of time to be away from each other for periods of time.

Many puppies, as well as some adult dogs, can become overwhelmed and unnecessarily frightened by two or three dogs trying to get access to them at the same time. In these instances, try sitting on the floor and holding your dog in your lap. If everything seems fine, let one dog interact, but continue to supervise. Then change dogs—putting the first dog away and allowing another dog to meet his new canine sibling.

Depending on your new dog's history, if he is nervous, shy, timid, fearful, or was bullied or intimidated by other dogs, or if your other dog likes to be in charge, you will need to take precautions and make introductions slowly. This process can take a few hours, days, or weeks. Never force introductions because this may destroy any chance of dogs getting along—ever! All introductions should be positive and stress free. Obviously, the situation itself dictates a certain amount of stress on the dogs' part, but your calm mannerisms and deportment will go a long way toward minimizing additional stress.

It may be necessary to put your new dog in an ex-pen and allow the dogs to meet and greet with a barrier between them. Sometimes learning to simply exist around each other is a huge step and a safe way for dogs to get comfortable in the same environment. Dogs who are nervous, anxious, disobedient, hyperactive, and so forth can create chaos and turmoil, which can lead to canine squabbling and scrapping. Use crates, x-pens, or room barriers to separate dogs when they can't be supervised.

If you are lucky enough to have an acre or two of fenced property and it's safe to let them run loose, then off-leash walks are great for letting dogs check out each other, explore their territory, run, play, and burn off excess stress and energy. Otherwise, parallel leash walks with your new dog and existing dog work well, too. They don't have to walk next to each other. One on each side of you works well, and, as they become more comfortable together, you can gradually close the distance.

Most problems arise because the new and existing dogs are allowed to run loose too quickly in a chaotic, stressful environment. When introductions do not go smoothly and a squabble ensues, there is a good chance the grudge and long-term distrust will continue. No one wants chaos and animosity between animals. So it is always worth taking the time to introduce animals slowly and properly. If you are uncertain, consult an experienced dog trainer or behaviorist. It is well worth the time and financial investment to establish a positive, stress-free environment from day one rather than trying to "fix" a bad situation.

Allow your new dog to explore his new house but keep an eye him.

"Better safe than sorry" is sound advice. So too is prevention! Prevention! Prevention!

In-Home Precautions

With any luck, the introductions will go off without a hitch, and you and your canine buddies will be on the fast track to plenty of fun and companionship. Allow the dogs to establish a hierarchy among themselves, with you, of course, being the leader. While it may be natural for owners to fuss and coo over the newest addition, it is important not to neglect your existing dog. First, it's neither fair nor nice, and doing so can inadvertently make some dogs resentful.

Allow your new dog to explore the house but stay close to him. Never allow him unlimited or unsupervised access to your home until you are certain how he will react. Once the home tour is complete, you may need to set up baby gates or ex-pens to corral his environment. Your newest addition may or may not be housetrained, and you don't want him hiking his leg from one end of the house to the other. Puppies, as well as a few adult dogs, love to chew on anything and everything—whether it fits in their mouth or not—which is another great reason to corral his environment.

In the beginning, you may need to pick up all toys, chew toys, bones, and any of your existing dog's favorite items to prevent any sibling rivalry or conflict. Introducing these items after the dogs have accepted each other is fine. However, not all dogs can live harmoniously with toys or chews lying around. Not all dogs are willing to lounge side by side gnawing on bones or treats. It may be that you need to keep them picked up at all times to avoid a power struggle. Separating dogs in crates or via baby gates while they are chewing bones also may be necessary.

How your new dog will react to his new home is difficult to say. Again, much will depend on his history, breed, temperament, personality, age, and his response to his new home. How you handle the situation is equally difficult to prescribe, and you may need to adjust or tweak the guidelines to suit your dog.

It's natural for many rescue dogs to be nervous or unsettled the first few days or weeks. Generally speaking, most dogs settle in after a short period of time. Calmness and patience on your part are most important and will go a long way toward helping your dog to adjust to his new life.

Introducing Children and Other Family Members

Children and dogs tend to go together, but too much togetherness all at one time can be overwhelming. Plenty of rescued dogs have never been around or socialized to children, and some dogs—well—simply do not tolerate any children, let alone noisy, rambunctious ones. Parents are the key figures when it comes to teaching children how to interact safely with a puppy or adult dog, and vice versa. By setting a few ground rules, you can help to ensure your children and new dog will develop a long-term friendship.

Young children are often boisterous and excitable and inconsistent with their behaviors. Often, their exuberance for the newest canine member can end up frightening rather than welcoming him. Many breeds, especially herding and terrier breeds, are excited by movement and like to chase and nip the legs of fleeing children. A natural doggie behavior, it's a common reason herding breeds are surrendered to shelters and rescue groups. Allowing these behaviors to be reinforced means you will end up with a dog who sees no harm in chasing, jumping up, or nipping. Also, like young dogs, children have short attention spans and easily lose their patience with a rambunctious, seemingly uncooperative dog, especially if that dog is jumping and nipping. Supervise

Supervise your newest canine addition and young children to discourage unwanted behaviors and create an environment of safe play.

your newest canine addition and young children to discourage unwanted behaviors and create an environment of safe play.

To prevent your dog from being overwhelmed, introduce family members one or two at a time in a calm, quiet manner. No yelling, squealing, screaming, or sudden movements. For puppies or small dogs, try having your children (as well as adults) sit or kneel on the floor, which is less intimidating. Otherwise, have them turn slightly sideway, avoid making direct eye contact, and let the dog approach on his terms.

Despite popular opinion, most dogs dislike hugging and petting on the head, which they often find annoying or frightening. Until you know how your dog will react, teach your children to scratch or pat his chest instead. Teach your children early on that your puppy or adult dog is not a toy but a living animal who must be handled properly and treated gently, kindly, and respectfully. Never allow children to overwhelm any dog or put him in a position where he can be bullied or frightened. Depending on your dog's temperament and personality, he may lash out and bite, and no one wants that.

Equally important, show older children how to properly pick up a small-breed dog or young puppy. For very young kids, do not allow them to pick up the dog without supervision. They can inadvertently hurt him should they pick him up by his ears or legs or, heaven forbid, drop him.

Keep in mind that most puppies and adult dogs have tons of energy, but they tire easily and need plenty of quiet time to recuperate from the demands of being a dog. Provide your new dog with a comfortable bed, crate, or ex-pen of his own for sleeping, recuperating, and escaping the domestic hustle and bustle. Everyone, especially children, should understand that all dogs need to be left alone while they are sleeping. No one wants a grumpy dog!

Introducing Cats

Chances are your existing dog and cat can learn to live harmoniously—even if they dislike each other. Your new dog also needs to learn that chasing, eating, or terrorizing the cat is unacceptable behavior that should be dropped immediately. To help set a positive relationship, provide your cat with plenty of escape routes. Cats like being up high, so provide plenty of access to countertops, furniture, and so forth. Also, provide your cat with a room of his own, such as a spare room, office, or den, so he can escape canine antics and not be bothered. For the first introduction, keep your new dog on leash so he can't chase or harass your cat (an ex-pen or baby gates also work well). You don't want your dog's first introduction to be a scratched nose! Depending on your dog's history, you will need to determine if he stands a chance of being safe around cats. The more dogs you keep together, the greater the chance they will switch to a pack mentality if they become overly excited. Some herding breeds, such as Border Collies, Australian Shepherds, and Belgian Tervurens like to stalk cats. So you'll want to be on the lookout for signs of this behavior and keep it under control. Allowing your dog to harass a cat or other animal is neither fair nor funny and should never be encouraged or tolerated. Always reward dogs and cats for behaving calmly in each other's presence.

Must Love Dogs...And Birds, Rabbits, Hamsters, and Other Critters

Some dogs are naturally gentle and calm around other animals, be they birds, rabbits, chickens, horses, or other companion animals. Stories have been told of dogs who developed the most unlikely best-friend relationships with horses, goats, sheep, chickens, and so forth. How your dog reacts around non-dog animals will greatly depend on his history, age, and whether or not his previous owner allowed him to develop unwanted habits. Chasing livestock is an instinctive behaviors for many dogs. In many areas, livestock owners are legally allowed to shoot a dog caught harassing their livestock. So taking the time to make your household a peaceable kingdom is well worth the effort. Follow these doable tips for keeping your animals safe:

- Make introductions slowly to allow plenty of time for your dog and the other animal to get used to each other. This may take several days or weeks.
- Keep your dog leashed and your bird, rabbit, hamster, or the like caged until you are absolutely certain they are both comfortable. Otherwise, depending on your dog's breed, history, instinct, and prey drive, the outcome may be disastrous.

Dogs and cats can learn to live together harmoniously.

- Choose a neutral area for introductions. For example, a room where your bird's cage is not normally located.
- Reward both dog and bird (or rabbit, ferret, etc.) for good behavior. (Be sure to have plenty of treats on hand before beginning your introductions.)
- Once your dog and other small pet become comfortable in the same room together, begin allowing your dog off leash as long as he continues to behave himself! Never leave your bird, rabbit, hamster, guinea pig, ferret in the same room unattended. Dogs are easily stimulated, and accidents can happen with even the most well-trained dog.

Horses

What's more fun than a trail ride with your best canine friend running alongside? While plenty of dogs do chase horses, and plenty of horses are fearful of dogs, in many cases, when precautions are taken, dogs and horses can learn to tolerate and even care for each other. Clashes between dogs and horses can quickly escalate into a dangerous situation for dog, horse, and rider. Therefore, a few doable precautions will keep everyone safe.

- Introduce your dog to horses at an early age and train/reward him for being calm. Ideally, this is easiest when puppies are young and impressionable. Depending on your dog's age and history and how he responds (i.e., fear or aggression), you may need to invest extra time and effort.

- Horses with positive experiences around dogs are ideal for introductions and socialization because they minimize the risk to dogs—especially puppies.
- If either animal is nervous, always work within their threshold by starting with enough distance between them so they can see each other, yet still take treats and respond to commands.
- Obedience train your dog—Come, Sit, Down, Stay, Wait—so you can preempt a chase or keep your dog safe should a horse panic, bolt, or become unruly.
- Keep your dog leashed and under control when around horses—especially if he lacks a solid, reliable recall (Come) command.
- Do not allow your dog to practice unwanted behaviors, such as barking or chasing horses. Some breeds are easily stimulated by movement (think herding dogs!), and a moving horse can easily excite a dog's natural prey or chase instinct.

Rescue Tip: COMMIT TO A FEW DAYS

Ideally, you will want to bring your newest addition home when you have a few days to spend together, such as the weekend. Otherwise, consider taking a few days off work to be home with the dogs. Although it may seem excessive, in the long run, it will help with the bonding process and to build a more solid human-canine relationship. Spending time together helps to ease some of the stress and anxiety your dogs may be feeling. You can monitor their behavior, learn about your new dog's habits, and intercept any potential problems. Doing so will help the transition, and your future time together will be much smoother.

Spending time with your new and existing dog is important. However, not everyone has the luxury of taking a few days or a week off to hang out with the dogs. In these instances, try to spend as much time with them as possible—especially when you're not working. For example, avoid scheduling activities during your nonwork hours—unless you plan to take your dogs with you! Same with vacations—try to avoid taking them and being away from your dogs for extended periods for the first few months. Again, it seems excessive, but the more time you can spend with your dogs, the smoother the transition and bonding process will be for you and the dogs.

Chapter 2

Socialization

Is there such a thing as too much cuteness? Not when you're a mixed-breed named Lily Bella, who melts your heart when you look at her. Her cute, intelligent face coupled with an elegant, compact sleekness makes you think there's a little (or a lot) of hound and terrier milling about in her DNA. This endearing little gal may not possess the characteristic "pit bull" brawn, but no doubt her inherited strength, tenacity, and intelligence kept her alive when she and her littermate brother were dumped and left to fend for themselves.

As is common in plenty of economically struggling communities, animals (especially dogs) are regularly and casually discarded at vacant lots, parks, or on roadsides. As with many strays, the process started with a telephone call to animal control: two puppies living under an abandoned house. Possibly someone moved away and left them behind, but the house appeared to have been abandoned for a good long time. Nothing indicated or hinted that their canine mom was ever present. Most mama dogs rarely leave their puppies unless it is in search of food, and even then they are seldom far away. No one recalls seeing a mama dog—ever. All evidence suggests that the littermates, barely old enough to be weaned, had been dumped. What happened to mama is anyone's guess. The potential scenarios are too heartbreaking to imagine.

How long the puppies had been on their own remains equally perplexing and elusive. Thin and sickly in appearance, the puppies should have been carefree bundles of sweetness romping in green grass and summer sun, yet their life was cowering under the house during the day and sneaking out at night to scavenge for food. With little or no human contact, a second animal control officer was called in to help corral and capture the terrified siblings. Lily Bella and her brother were not truly feral, but rather stray dogs who lacked any socialization skills and were merely shifting to survival mode. Identified as Pit Bull mixes, the

LILY BELLA IS A PIT BULL MIX WHO WAS FOUND AS A STRAY.

skeptical puppies, newest members of an animal shelter environment, faced an insurmountable uphill battle. ("Pit Bull" is not a breed but rather a generic term that encompasses several dog breeds whose original purpose included bull and bear baiting and, later, dog fighting. It is loosely applied to breeds with similar traits and characteristics.) Lily Bella's refined, streamlined physique suggests a wedge of Whippet or Greyhound may be coursing through her pedigree. At four months old, this running machine's speed and agility paint a fair picture of the modern-day breed. Even so, would her "Pit Bull" connection keep her from being rescued?

LILY BELLA AND TYLER BONDED INSTANTLY.

Many counties in California have high-kill shelters, with an estimated 85 to 90 percent of stray and surrendered dogs being euthanized. Scared, skittish, or fearful dogs are seldom given an opportunity to prove their worth. Pit Bulls are rampant in California's central San Joaquin valley, and euthanasia remains routine for those entering the system.

Lady Luck's giant beacon shone brightly on the two siblings. Rather than being picked up by county animal control where they faced an almost certain sad fate, they ended up at Tulare Animal Services, a municipal facility with a roughly 55 percent euthanasia rate—a low number for many California shelters. The siblings' guardian angel was Tammy Burrows, rescue coordinator, who saw potential in the two strays and was determined to save them. They would not become another statistic on her watch.

Two weeks after being hauled out from under an abandoned house, and now in what must have seemed like the pampered life with a warm bath, yummy food, and a cozy bed, the sweet puppies were slowly coming around and starting to trust humans. At roughly eight to ten weeks of age, the puppies' narrow window of socialization remained open. Plenty of handling, playing, and cuddling helped to begin instilling confidence and trust. No doubt the turkey, cheese, and chicken-infused bribery helped a lot, too!

Tulare Animal Services takes in upwards of thirty dogs per day, mostly Chihuahuas and Pit Bulls. Walk down any street, and stray dogs run unchecked. Want a dog? Pick one off the street. No one adopts from the shelters. For Lily Bella and her littermate, the best chance

at a successful future meant relocating them from the agricultural region to the Pacific Northwest. Dawn Rennie, founder of Enzo's Acres, a nonprofit rescue organization in Portland, transported them to Oregon, where they were placed in a foster home.

Certified veterinary technician Bobbi Smith was working the day the siblings were brought into South Willamette Veterinary Clinic for spaying and neutering. Smith, along with her husband Todd and four-year-old son Tyler, had been talking about rescuing another dog. Lily Bella, the more outgoing of the two siblings, could not have been more perfect.

Puppies learn an amazing array of essential manners and important survival skills from their canine mama during their first eight weeks of life. A mama dog's swift and fair rewards and punishments let a puppy know not to be cheeky, or bite too hard, or fight with his canine siblings; to play gently; to wait his turn; to listen and to stay put or rally around her when told to do so. Behavioral challenges can be an issue when removing puppies from their canine mother too early. In this instance, no options were available. That decision had been made by whoever abandoned them.

A bit skittish and a little scared for the first few days but showing no signs of aggression, Lily Bella bonded instantly with Tyler, and the two remain inseparable. "Mommy I love her and want her to be my dog! She can sleep with me and scare the monsters away!"

Recognizing the importance of socialization, especially considering the absence of a mama dog, as well as Lily Bella's possible terrier/hound heritage, the Smiths understood that the responsibility of teaching social skills and life manners fell on them. They started straightaway preparing Lily Bella for all of the exciting adventures that lie ahead. Not wanting to overwhelm the little gal by teaching her everything at once, they established priorities, including introducing and socializing her to everything she is likely to encounter as an adult dog.

Lily Bella's new life as an avid outdoor hiking, backpacking, camping, and all-round perfect pet companion already includes a week-long backpacking/camping trip. Avid outdoor enthusiasts, the Smiths already include Doberman Pinscher Chiefy in their wilderness outings and plan to include Lily Bella, as well.

Remarkably, this little gal of unknown heritage who was terrified of humans shows no residual skittishness. Friendly, outgoing, dignified, lively, and affectionate, this once abandoned puppy facing an almost certain terrible fate now lives the high life, surrounded by love, guidance, and direction, with a future as bright and beautiful as her endearing spirit.

Socialization: The Key to a Dog's Future

In a perfect world, all puppies would grow into adult dogs who are friendly, outgoing, and emotionally stable. In the real world, many puppies and adult dogs, be they purebred or mixed breeds, come with baggage we may never fully understand. Some dogs, like Lily Bella, get the worst start in life but blossom into wonderful cherished companions. Other dogs get the best start in life but are traumatized by owner ignorance, stupidity, or unforeseen circumstances.

Why do some dogs flourish while others falter?

Behavior always comes from a combination of genetics and environment, so much depends on a dog's breeding. Some dogs can experience negligent, even abusive conditions, and still mature into emotionally sound adult dogs because of superior genetics. Lily Bella and her brother lived an isolated life under an abandoned building with no mama dog or human guidance, yet because of some proper socialization at the tail end of the critical socialization period, and an apparently amazing set of genes, they are quickly developing and maturing into great companions.

For every dog like Lily Bella, there are countless dogs whose compromised conditions and deprivation early in life result in their inability to tolerate change. They are more likely to develop fearful reactions to people, noises, and unfamiliar locations. They tend to be more cautious, shy, fearful, and frequently nervous, avoiding or retreating from unfamiliar objects or situations. As adult dogs, they usually find it more difficult to cope with new or stressful situations.

If your dog came from a less than ideal environment, he may already avoid people, become easily fearful or timid much of the time, or show signs of aggression. If this is the

Training Tip: YOUR DOG'S FUTURE

According to the National Council on Pet Population Study and Policy, behavioral problems such as aggression, fear, timidity, and the like, which frequently correlate with lack of socialization, are a common reason many dogs are abandoned or surrendered to animal shelters. Evidence clearly shows that early socialization can prevent the onset of these serious canine problems. If you do nothing else for your dog, you owe it to him to make the time to properly and adequately socialize him during this critical life stage. Doing so is time-consuming and takes a lot of energy. However, his future well-being depends on how much you do—or fail to do—during this critical period.

case, you have zero time to lose. You may want to retain the assistance of a smart trainer or behaviorist to make up for lost ground. Although he may never become the dog he could have been, you can help to improve the situation by teaching him life skills and providing him with plenty of experiences to help build his confidence and bravery.

It's worth mentioning that while much of this chapter is geared toward puppies, most, if not all, the information can be applied to adult dogs, too. How quickly your dog progresses will depend on his age, breed, genetics, his emotional and physical state, and what type of life you envision him living. It may not be easy, but patience, love, understanding, and a lot of baby steps will keep you moving in the right direction. Five steps forward, three steps backward—and you're still two steps ahead!

The Environmental Component of Socialization

Keep in mind that not all aggressive or fearful dogs have "bad" genes. Plenty of dogs are afraid of people because they were not properly socialized as young puppies. This is not uncommon on ranches and farms where working dogs live an isolated life, seeing few, if any, people during the critical socialization period. These dogs are not necessarily hardwired to be shy or fearful of people, but because of their lack of socialization, they often view unfamiliar people as a threat.

Lily Bella is a good example of how genes (nature) and development and learning (nurture) play important roles in a dog's future. (Also known as the nature versus nurture debate.) Had her situation been different (i.e., had she been well socialized), it's hard to believe she would have been a terrified eight-week-old puppy cowering under an abandoned house. Had she not been rescued when she had, had she continued to live as a stray, it's highly likely her fear would have become more deeply ingrained, thereby increasing the difficulty of a successful rehabilitation. Yet, her superior genes no doubt allowed her to overcome her once fearful behavior.

These rescued Border Collies prove that good socialization and training can work miracles!

We know from the pioneering work of John Paul Scott and John L. Fuller that both genetic and environmental influences impact the development of canine behavior. One of their most important contributions is the description of sensitive periods in the social development of dogs, with the "socialization" period being the critical time between three and twelve weeks of age. (Some experts say three to fourteen to sixteen weeks.) It's the time frame in a puppy's life when "a small amount of experience will produce a great effect on later behavior."

What Is Socialization?

Socialization is incredibly important, but what is it? Trainers have all sorts of definitions, but in the simplest of terms it is about classical conditioning: creating an association between two stimuli. This is a learning process in which your puppy is exposed—in a safe, positive, and nonthreatening way—to all of the things he is likely to encounter as an adult dog, such as other animals, the clapping of hands, elevators, stairs, vacuums, trash cans, kids on bicycles, women in floppy hats, and so forth.

That said, somewhere along the way, socialization became synonymous with a giant free-for-all. Taking your dog to the park and allowing him to be bombarded by other animals, strange sights, weird noises, and hordes of screaming, rambunctious kids grabbing at him, stepping on him, or squealing at him is *not* a positive experience. Likewise, taking him to a puppy class and allowing him to be mauled, bullied, or sent yelping by bigger, bossier, more dominant puppies is not a positive experience, either. Granted, some puppies may not be affected, but the majority of them will suffer in the long run. These types of experiences can permanently traumatize a young dog.

You want your puppy's association with his world—everything and anything he is likely to encounter as an adult dog—to be positive so he grows up thinking life is good and safe. This point cannot be stressed enough. Puppies need to play and interact with other puppies, and even adult dogs, yet that is a teeny, tiny piece of their education, not the only piece. Every second of the day, you are either adding to or subtracting from the human-canine relationship. Dog training, which includes socialization, is all about the relationship you have with your dog. Protecting that relationship should be priority one.

Thankfully, it is not difficult to find lots of fun places and ways to socialize your puppy.

You want your puppy's encounters with the outside world to be safe and positive.

How to Socialize Your Dog

As soon as he is adequately vaccinated, you should take him for plenty of kisses and cookies everywhere that is safe and where dogs are permitted, such as:

- Outdoor cafes
- Shopping centers
- Hardware stores
- Banks
- Coffee shops
- Flower shops
- Horse barns
- Veterinarian's office

Expose him to a wide variety of people including toddlers, teenagers, people in wheelchairs, and men in uniform. Expose him to other animals, such as cats, horses, chickens, and furry or feathered pets. If the goats are scary, let him sit in your lap. Pick fresh fruit and let him savor the sweet taste of berries. Make the clapping of hands, the jingling of keys, and the clatter of dog bowls no big deal. Teach him to walk and play on different surfaces, such as gravel, grass, sandy beaches, vinyl and tile floors, and so forth. Don't forget bridges with varying planks of wood or metal.

How about a fun bicycle ride with your rescue?

Take him on elevators and escalators, and expose him to open stairs, closed stairs, steep stairs, narrow stairs, wood stairs, and grated stairs (watch his toes and be careful he doesn't fall). Expose him to paper bags blowing in the wind, honking horns, garden hoses, sprinklers, wind chimes, and everything else he might come in contact with as an adult dog. Let him play in and around empty boxes, tunnels, and buckets. Allow him to investigate trees, rocks, bushes, branches, leaves, and fallen fruit. Take him to the beach and let him climb on driftwood and dig in the sand. Go for a hike in the woods and let him climb on and over fallen trees. Take him someplace new every day.

Give him a ride in a wheelbarrow or bundle him up in your jacket and take him for a bicycle ride. Buy him a lifejacket and take him boating or kayaking. Let him go swimming with a slow, fun introduction to lakes, rivers, and pools. Push him around pet-friendly stores in a shopping cart. Sit him in your lap while you gently swing on a swing or stretch out in a hammock.

Teach him the art of walking past people without always having to say hello. Teach him to potty on different surfaces—grass, gravel, dirt, asphalt, as well as on and off leash. (You'll appreciate this one when traveling and stopping for potty breaks.) Challenge his mind by teaching him to problem solve, such as how to find and retrieve his ball from under a chair, how to dig the marrow out of a bone, how to balance and walk on a plank or log, how to climb over a downed tree that's bigger than he thinks he can climb.

Attend a small puppy class—preferably with not more than three or four puppies—or invite friends and neighborhood kids over (after they have washed their hands and left

If your dog is afraid of a particular person, do not force him to engage.

their shoes at the door) for kisses and supervised play. Take him walking with one friend and her dog. Handle him multiple times a day cuddling, kissing, and whispering sweet nothings in his ear.

Balancing Act

Socializing your dog is a balancing act. You must expose him to the world around him while simultaneously protecting him from potentially harmful or fearful situations, yet being careful about encouraging or rewarding fearful behaviors. You want to find a balance between the right amount of exposure and stimulation, while still providing a safe, stress-free environment. Try really hard to avoid exposing him to a barrage of constant noise and stimulation every waking moment. Puppies have short attention spans, and they need plenty of down time to sleep and recover from their busy day of being a puppy. When they are awake, however, they need enough physical and mental stimulation and socialization to grow into healthy, happy adult dogs.

Finding that balance will depend on your dog. Understanding the innate characteristics of your dog's breed is especially handy during this time. You will need to read his body language by observing his reactions to different situations. Watch his ears and tail and body posture. Is he happy? Fearful? Apprehensive? Courageous? Inquisitive?

Submissive? By understanding and reading your dog's body language, you will be able to assess his comfort level and evaluate or adjust the situation accordingly. Here are a few examples:

- If your dog is afraid of vacuum cleaners, leave it in the corner of the room and let him adjust to its presence on his own terms. Leave a few tasty treats next to it and let him figure out how to get them on his own. Another option is to turn it on in another room. If possible, have someone turn it on in another room while your praise and reward your dog with plenty of yummy cookies. (Don't confuse a dog's innate or quirky behaviors, such as attacking a vacuum, with fear. These are two different situations that require different approaches.)
- If your dog is afraid of a particular person, do not force him to engage. Simply allow him to sort it out on his terms. Have the person sit on the floor, which is less intimidating than standing over a puppy, and reward him with treats when he approaches on his own.
- If your dog is not used to children, a room full of rambunctious children may be overwhelming or downright scary. Ideally, you should modify or restrict the exposure to one quiet, well-behaved child in the beginning until your dog is confident enough to handle more.

Comforting or Coddling?

A good deal of controversy surrounds the topic of comforting or soothing fearful dogs. Certainly, it's human nature to want to comfort a fearful dog, but does coddling or

Did You Know? SOCIALIZATION AND VACCINATIONS

Although vaccinations are important to your puppy, so too is socialization. A hotly debated topic is the perceived risk of exposing puppies (or insufficiently vaccinated adult dogs) to other dogs prior to completing their full complement of vaccinations at around sixteen weeks. Some veterinarians adamantly oppose socialization before sixteen weeks of age because of the risk of contracting an infectious disease, such as parvovirus. The decision is a personal one and should always be made in consultation with your veterinarian. Plenty of opportunities exist to safely socialize your puppy, but until he is fully vaccinated, avoid those public places where the risk of encountering infected dogs is high, such as dog parks, pet-supply stores, and large puppy or obedience classes.

LITTLE-DOG SYNDROME IS NOT FUNNY

Differences exist between a well-behaved puppy who you indulge and a spoiled ruffian who bites and snaps at people. Labeled "little-dog syndrome," this spoiled behavior tends to be seen more often in small or toy dogs. People tend to be amused by snarky behaviors in little dogs, such as a pampered Pomeranian sitting on his owner's lap and growling at passersby or a four-pound Chihuahua sprinting to attack someone's shin bone. You have probably caught yourself laughing at these situations, too. Some owners think the behavior is amusing, so they reward it, whether intentionally or not. Sadly, these behaviors are dangerous because they become ingrained, and these puppies grow into adult dogs who think they are invincible. It is nearly impossible to turn these half-pint hooligans into nice, happy dogs. Instead, these puppies grow into dogs who can't be trusted and really aren't fun to be around. Look ahead to your puppy's future and recognize those behaviors you want to encourage and discourage so that you can instill and reward those behaviors that foster a happy, healthy puppy.

otherwise rewarding a dog who shows fear reinforce that fear? For years, the accepted theory has been that if a dog is fearful and you attempt to comfort him by saying, "It's ok honey. Don't be afraid. Mommy won't let anything happen to you," then you are rewarding his fearful actions, which inadvertently compounds the situation by reinforcing his fear.

Fear is designed to be aversive, and many behaviorist believe that comforting a noise-sensitive dog who goes into freak-out mode at the sound of thunder or fireworks is not going to reinforce his fear. Calmly stroking his ears, scratching his belly, or talking in a soothing voice probably won't make him worse. According to certified applied animal behaviorist Patricia McConnell, PhD, "Fear is an emotion, and 'reinforcement' refers to something than increases a behavior. You can't, technically, reinforce an emotion, but you can increase the frequency of a particular behavior."

It's no surprise that studies support both sides of the issue. However, McConnell goes on to explain that if stroking and petting a dog who is fearful of thunder has a positive effect, and the dog is no longer pacing, panting, and whining, then maybe rubbing his belly isn't such a bad thing.

That said, scolding or correcting a fearful or apprehensive dog will definitely exacerbate the situation.

On the other hand, if your dog yelps because you accidently stepped on his foot, coddling him may reinforce some fearful or wimpy behavior. Instead, in these instances, immediately play with him and talk to him in a happy voice. This takes his mind off the situation and puts his focus on your happy, positive energy.

Temperament and its Limitations

Puppies and adult dogs are unique individuals and must be treated as such. By understanding as much as possible about the breed you have chosen, you will have an easier time understanding why he does what he does and, subsequently, how best to manage his behavior during the socialization process. For example, many dogs are attracted to moving objects, which incite their chase instinct. By exposing your puppy to these objects, including strollers, wheelchairs, shopping cars, vacuums, bicycles, and kids on roller blades and skateboards, your puppy is less likely to have an issue with them as he gets older. Of course, for some dogs, especially herding and terrier breeds, chasing moving objects is in their DNA, and you will need to work hard to curtail this potentially dangerous behavior.

Some dogs are prone to developing obsessive-compulsive behaviors, including Doberman Pinschers, German Shepherds, Dalmatians, Rottweilers, and Border Collies, to name a few. So, during the socialization process—and throughout the dog's life—try your best to prevent these behaviors from developing or, at the very least, from continuing. For instance, never allow your puppy to fixate on cats or other animals, chase his tail, chase shadows, or run fence lines. And never, ever use laser lights to play with your dog. Although it may seem like a fun way to exercise your puppy, laser-light games can create stress, anxiety, and potentially life-threatening obsessive behaviors in many dogs.

If your puppy has a bad experience at a young age, it is imperative that you address the situation right away while the socialization window is still open. Do not be fooled into thinking your puppy will grow out of his phobias. Once behaviors like fear or aggression become ingrained, they are more difficult, if not impossible, to eliminate and fix. The socialization period is the best time to address any perceived problems. If your puppy is showing signs of anything other than normal puppy behaviors, this is the time to seek advice from a smart trainer or behaviorist who can help to repair the damage.

Chapter 3

Body Language

TAKE A "CHANCE" ON A $20,000 PIT BULL

Take a chance is exactly what Brightside Animal Center and Judy Anderson did when they opened their hearts to a Pit Bull who was found severely injured, dehydrated, and near death in July 2013 near Terrebonne, Oregon. Whether he jumped, fell, or was intentionally pushed out of the car window was unclear at that time, but those in the know say he survived being dragged at 45 to 50 miles per hour (72 to 80 kph) for roughly 4 to 5 miles (6 to 8 km). For 72 hours Chance, so named because of his incredible will to survive and his second chance at life, lay near death on the side of a dusty, sagebrush-lined highway as the temperature hovered at 95°F (35°C) in Oregon's high desert. Picked up by the sheriff's department and taken to a local veterinary clinic, his injuries were so extensive euthanasia was scheduled if no owner came forward.

His history is sketchy, but it's believed Chance was bred in Central Oregon and sold to a lady who eventually could no longer keep him. Via a Craigslist ad, Chance was sold or given to a young man, but who was driving the car from which he was dragged is hazy. No charges were filed, and the sheriff's department later determined it to be an accident. However, facing staggering veterinary bills, the owner quickly surrendered Chance.

As seems to be the case with so many rescued dogs, Chance would not go easily across the Rainbow Bridge. Chance had come to stay, and life seemed to have a plan of its own for the half black, half white, 100 percent handsome Pit Bull. He was moved to Brightside Animal Center a few miles down the road, where he would receive 24-hour care. Control his pain and euthanize him later, euthanize him

DONATIONS TO BRIGHTSIDE ANIMAL CENTER HELPED PAY FOR CHANCE'S MANY VETERINARY EXPENSES.

immediately, or treat his injuries and try to save him were the immediate options. "Anyone who saw Chance realized once we started on him, we were in it for the long haul," says Chris Bauersfeld, Brightside's executive director. With a 98 percent save rate, Chance was in good hands but not out of the woods. Brightside's high-save philosophy is what drove the staff to pull out all the veterinary stops for Chance. (It's something they do for all the animals that are brought to them.) Infection had started to set in, but it was determined he could be saved. Within one hour of arriving at Brightside, Chance was in surgery. He faced multiple major surgical procedures, countless bandage changes, a long course of medications to combat infection and pain, and months of treatment and recovery time. During one procedure, his heart stopped, and the veterinarian worked hard to bring him back. Today, all that is behind him.

TODAY, CHANCE IS AS WONDERFUL A FRIEND AS HIS ADOPTER COULD HOPE FOR.

His face is that of an angel. His eyes soft and kind, stare out from pictures posted on Facebook. His body covered in bandages, his head cradled in a head cone, and a goofy t-shirt protecting his sensitive skin tell his story and convince people around the world of the beauty to be found in a rescued Pit Bull. Half black. Half white. One-hundred percent heartthrob. Donations from as far away as the United Kingdom, Australia, and Russia poured in to help offset his veterinary and hospitalization expenses, which are estimated at $20,000.

Six months after Brightside first laid hands on Chance, one journey ended and another began. Judy Anderson, Brightside's trainer, who had been fostering Chance for several months, adopted the charming Pit Bull who epitomizes a breed that is goofy, honest, courageous, and would gladly give its life for yours.

Today, Chance is an ambassador for a much maligned breed, and as good and true a friend as Anderson could wish for. His tremendous will to survive, love of life, and positive attitude endear him to everyone who crosses his path. With patience, consistency, and positive reinforcement, Chance is learning to control and channel his exuberance for life.

For several months before and after his adoption, Chance had nightmares—often crying, whining, and shrieking in his sleep. Granted, no scientific data exists (yet!) that proves dogs have nightmares. However, based on observation, it stands to reason that dogs do have nightmares and possibly experience some sort of posttraumatic stress disorder (PTSD), which of course, is a hotly debated topic in cafes, taverns, and veterinary clinics around the globe.

Chance's spirit, intelligence, and gentle heart never faltered from his ordeal. Riding in the car remains one of his favorite adventures. His daily visits to Brightside as the center's self-appointed breed ambassador and Anderson's colleague and training partner brings a smile to everyone he encounters. "He is the quintessential Pit Bull—confident, sensitive, loves people, and gets along well with other dogs and cats," says Anderson. "He communicates to me when another dog does not have good energy." Chance's communication skills are profound, and his keen ability to read another dog's emotional temperature makes him a master at calming reactive dogs, be they aggressive, stressed, or just flexing their muscles. Could he be so smart that he simply pretends the transgression never occurred? Whether he is helping Anderson at Brightside Animal Center, hiking in the woods, playing in the park, or walking around downtown Bend, his natural ability to defuse a tense or potentially disastrous situation makes him an incredibly complex canine. Chance's job is not simple, but he certainly makes it look that way.

Anderson hopes Chance's legacy will be that his will to survive had a purpose. He helps Anderson. He helps other dogs. He brought together people from around the world to help with a common cause. Most of these people Chance will never meet, yet his admirers undoubtedly feel a connection to him and a soul that is gentle, grand, and invincible.

Breeds traditionally used as livestock guarding dogs may be reserved with strangers.

Decoding a Dog's Body Language

"If only my dog could talk, he could tell me what he's thinking!" How many times have you said that or heard someone else say it? Sure, owners often anthropomorphize—attribute human characteristics to nonhuman animals—and that's not necessarily a bad thing—but dogs are not little people in fuzzy suits. Just because a dog looks guilty doesn't mean he is guilty. Dogs have their own specialized communication system, and what you think they are communicating may be a long way from what is really happening.

Scientific research has increased our knowledge of how dogs think and feel. Progressive trainers and animal behaviorists all seem to concur that dogs have emotions and feelings. Yet, absent mental telepathy or a scientific breakthrough, the truth of the matter is that what dogs are really saying when they bark or growl or what they are thinking when they cock their head at a piece of lint will always remain a bit speculative.

Generally speaking, dogs are much more adept at reading body language than humans are at reading dogs (or people!). Dogs are capable of zoning in on the slightest change in our deportment, such as a change in our breathing or tone of voice, a sigh, pursed lips, slumped shoulders, a shift in our body weight, and so forth.

We can't get into a dog's head; therefore, we can never know for certain what he is thinking, just as we can never know with absolute certainty what another human being is thinking. Dogs can't talk to us with words, but they can give us a pretty good idea of what they are thinking and feeling by communicating with us through their own specialized communication system. By studying a lot of different dogs in different situations, experts

Evaluating dogs in a shelter environment is dicey even for the most experienced trainer because most dogs, although certainly not all, are nervous, worried, or anxious, with many dogs shutting down emotionally or reverting to the fight-or-flight mode. Getting a true reading on a dog's temperament/personality means evaluating him on neutral territory where he's comfortable being himself. Yet, shelters are anything but neutral. They're often cold, noisy, chaotic environments, and the energy is completely overwhelming for most dogs, which makes evaluating them difficult. While they do their very best, not all shelter employees or volunteers are trained to evaluate dogs in stressful situations.

Can you recognize the signs of a stressed dog? Depending on the breed, temperament, personality, sex, and history, stressed dogs in a shelter environment (or any environment) may exhibit these common signs:

- Hyperactivity
- Pacing
- Pawing
- Vomiting
- Coughing
- Drooling
- Barking
- Sneezing
- Yawning
- Shaking/Trembling
- Whining
- Leaving damp footprints

Some stressed dogs emotionally shut down, freezing in place, backing away from activity, hiding, tucking tail, refusing to eat, drink, or interact.

A key component of a successful adoption is recognizing that your rescued dog may need a few days or weeks (or longer) to adjust to his new home—thereby allowing his true personality to shine.

have built a mosaic of knowledge and a pretty detailed picture of a dog's body language, expressions, and actions that help us to decode what dogs are most likely thinking or feeling. By studying the signals dogs use with each other, you increase your ability to communicate with your dog, as well as with most dogs. Imagine being able to read your dog, or any dog, as well as he reads you!

What's His Purpose?

If you know your breed's history, origin, and the job for which he was originally bred, you can use this information to help decode his communication system. This point cannot be stressed enough. Before you throw up your hands and say, "He's just a dog!"— consider that dogs were bred for a specific purpose. Some breeds, for example, have a characteristic grin in which they raise their upper lip and expose their teeth. A goofy, friendly behavior that is frequently, although incorrectly, mistaken as an aggressive baring of the teeth. Experts can't say for certain what emotion "grinning" dogs are expressing, but their body language, which is wiggly and friendly with squinty eyes, tells you they probably aren't contemplating any aggressive thoughts. On the other hand, some dogs who have been trained on electric collars will expose their teeth in a grin-like gesture while occasionally snapping at the air as a means of displacing the stress and anxiety caused by these type of collars. These two similar-looking behaviors communicate different messages, and understanding the difference will save you and your dog a good deal of grief.

Also, years ago, many herding breeds did double duty as protectors and watchdogs on the farm. Therefore, sights and sounds and nuances that might be lost on, say, a Bulldog, are likely to attract the attention of a herding dog. Subsequently, for many of these breeds, the correct temperament is not to be overly welcoming to everyone they meet, but rather reserved with strangers but not shy. Owners or trainers who do not understand the history, origin, and temperament of a breed may inadvertently misread the dog's body language and hold it against him. To better understand your dog, it's important to recognize and value the history, origin, and traits specific to your chosen breed.

For mixed breeds or rescued dogs in whom the history or breed is unknown, you may have to be satisfied with attempting to identify the breed-specific characteristics of purebred dogs, such as size, coat type, tail set, behavioral traits, and the like that may shed some light on what breeds might be milling about in your dog's DNA makeup. More often than not, these are usually educated guesses because although your dog may look like a Labrador Retriever he might just behave like a Basenji, as evidenced by the famous Scott and Fuller study of genetics and dog behavior.

Finding the Meaning

An understanding of canine communication is a good beginning to any relationship with a dog. An exact translation isn't always possible, but it is good to consider what the dog might be saying. Familiarizing yourself with the multiple meanings of tail wags, averted gazes, and other signals will help provide you with a better understanding of what your dog is trying to communicate, such as his mood, his comfort level in a given situation, and his reaction to changes in his environment. Developing this skill will help make your dog's life and training more enjoyable and avoid some, but not all, unpleasant misunderstandings.

Decoding your dog's body language takes a bit of practice and can be tricky because dogs, like people, are all different. Some dogs are harder to read than others. Dogs with hair that hangs in their eyes or stands at attention all the time or dogs with cropped ears and docked tails can be more challenging to read. Also, dogs often communicate with signals that can have multiple meanings, change rapidly, and can be specific to a situation. For example, a wagging tail is not always the sign of a happy dog. Yawning can signify stress or be an appeasement or calming signal that tells another dog, "I'm not going to bother you" or "I don't want any trouble." Likewise, a dog may roll over on his back to expose his chest and belly to an approaching dog or human but react negatively when a human misinterprets the behavior as an invitation to scratch his belly. The dog may be exposing his belly as a submissive behavior—to indicate he poses no threat—but would really like the intruder to go away or leave him alone. One owner recounted a story of how her dog "took down a young black Lab," which she interpreted as aggression on the part of her dog. In actuality, the black Lab was being submissive, rolling onto his back, and telling the woman's dog, "I want no trouble."

People expect dogs to be something they're not. Some dogs are conflicted. Others have difficulty trusting humans or other animals. Some dogs wag their tails, offering cues of inviting closeness from strangers, but when strangers get too close, they feel overwhelmed and try to scare them away. Some dogs seem to solicit human contact but make it abundantly clear that they have mixed feelings about meeting new people. Others have a scary bark but welcome the approach of strangers.

Understanding canine body language will go a long way toward helping you to know when to correct or when to shrug off a behavior. This chapter will provide you with

A dog may roll over on his back as a submissive gesture.

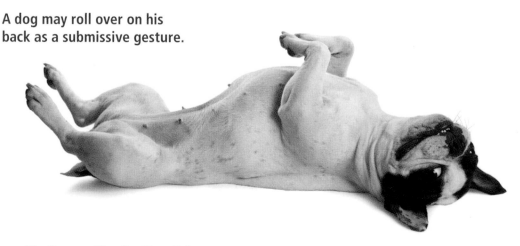

Dogs often prevent altercations through body language:
Photo 1—A terrier and Golden Retriever approach each other and their body language conveys confidence and curiosity; **Photo 2**—They sniff each other; **Photo 3**—A Nova Scotia Duck Tolling Retriever approaches cautiously; **Photo 4**—They all go their own way without incident.

plenty of useful information in getting started. However, it is not ironclad or written in stone. These are guidelines because dogs, like people, are different, and canine behavior is fluid. It changes in the blink of an eye. A dog may feel happy one second and fearful the next. Work on expanding your canine skills by spending as much time as possible observing dogs interacting together and with other people. Dog parks are ideal for scrutinizing plenty of canine signals. Consider videotaping the dogs so you can play back and watch in slow motion.

Communication Is Essential

Relationships are based on communication. A mutual communication system connects you to others, be it other people or animals, and feeling connected is an integral part of any good relationship. Canine body language is pretty universal. You can travel anywhere in the world and, for the most part, all dogs speak the same language. Once you understand a dog's communication system, you can communicate with almost any dog. How fabulous is that?

Problems arise when owners expect dogs to understand their ever-changing rules and endless verbal commands, but they fail to take into account that dogs don't speak human. (This is one of those areas where anthropomorphizing can get you into trouble.) Yes, dogs can learn *Sit, Come, Stay, Stand, Rollover, Wave,* and a dozen other cues, but expecting a dog to understand, "Why did you potty on the carpet?" Or "I'm so mad at you! Why didn't you come when I called you?" will only undermine the human-canine relationship. Since the smartest dog in the world will never master a human language, the responsibility of becoming bilingual rests squarely upon your shoulders. For the human-canine relationship to flourish, you need to learn to speak dog, so to speak.

Reading body language is something most humans do every day. Granted, with the explosion of social media, the process of nonverbal communication is in danger of becoming a bit of a lost art. (Think of how comments posted online are quickly and easily misinterpreted because, without body language, it's difficult, if not impossible, to read the person's true intent.) When you look into someone's eyes, you know whether they are attentive, happy, sad, irritated. By reading subtle and not-so-subtle signals, such as posture, gesture, breathing, and energy, you know when a person is agitated, aggressive, friendly, happy, honest, stretching the truth, and so forth. Their body language tells you when you can push your luck a little more or when you should drop the subject immediately. The same concept applies to dogs. Thankfully, dogs are not yet hiding their body language behind computers, texts, emails, and Facebook or Twitter posts and tweets. Once you understand the universal language of dogs, you are well on your way to improving the human-canine relationship.

The Sum of the Parts

A dog's body parts tell you a lot about what he is thinking or feeling. The positioning of his ears, eyes, mouth, head, or tail will give you a pretty good idea of what's going on in his brain. That said, each body part has to be taken in context with the dog's overall body posture. For example, a dog wags his tail, but is his body shifted forward or backward?

Training Tip: OBSERVE YOUR DOG

Watch your dog when he is sleeping, playing, eating, interacting with other people and dogs, and so forth. See if you pick up on any of the body language cues listed on the following pages.

Some behaviorists refer to this as a dog's "energy." Just as Chance, the rescued Pit Bull, lets Anderson know when another dog's energy is not good, you too can tune in to what a dog is telling you. Generally speaking, dogs whose bodies are shifted forward are displaying a sign of friendliness, which usually includes a full or partial body wiggle. These dogs usually welcome a giant love fest of kisses and belly rubs. The dogs whose bodies are stiff and immobile, mouth closed, and tail wagging only at the tip, usually requires a bit of caution when approaching. Rather than kneeling down with arms wide open, you may need to stand your ground but without adding additional tension. On the other hand, when dogs direct their "energy" backward, most often they are on the defense and fearful. If approached, they may bite.

So you can see that the positioning of the dog's body, be it forward or backward, coupled with the positioning of his ears, tail, mouth, legs, and more can help you to predict his future behavior.

Recognizing body language and what it means is important because it helps you to help your dog. Knowing when he is stressed or anxious or playful rather than aggressive is always a good thing. True, mastering canine body language can be overwhelming at first. If that's the case, focus on one or two body parts in the beginning. Perhaps you have already noticed some signals your dog is using, such as a tongue flick or yawning. As you become more proficient at reading one body cue, move onto another part, such as head tilts or head turns.

Although this is a simplified look at a very complicated topic, it will help to get you thinking about what your dog might be thinking. Once you start looking for emotional cues, you'll see them everywhere. Once you start recognizing them, you will be amazed at how obvious they are to read.

Ears

Ear size, shape, and carriage vary enormously from breed to breed and even from dog to dog within the same breed. The names can seem a bit quirky, too, such as the English Toy Terrier whose ear shape is referred to as "candle flame ears." Or the "button ears" of the Fox Terrier or Irish Terrier. Some Shetland Sheepdogs have "cocked" ears, whereas the Bedlington Terrier has "filbert-shaped ears." Some breeds, such as the Whippet have "flying" ears, whereas the Welsh Springer Spaniel has "vine-leaf" ears. Hounds usually have drop or pendulous ears, whereas the German Shepherd Dog, Belgian Malinois, and Siberian Husky usually have erect ears. Ear set is part and parcel of a breed's history and origin and the job for which it was originally bred. Knowing your dog's normal ear set will help you to decode when something might be array.

- Ears hanging relaxed, coupled with a relaxed tail, indicate a neutral or comfortable state.
- Ears forward (perked up ears) and the head tilted to one side usually indicate curiosity, excitement, playfulness, confidence, or interest.

This Australian Shepherd's ear position and facial tension indicate that he is not comfortable with the Border Collie's close proximity. Once the Border Collie looks away, the Aussie relaxes slightly.

- Ears tensely drawn forward, coupled with a lowered head, can indicate confidence and/or guarding. Can also indicate a predatory/stalking position in which a chase is about to begin.
- Ears pulled back, close to the head indicate tension or fear. Can also indicate an attempt to calm or cut off any interaction with another dog, depending on the accompanying body posture.

Eyes

Like a dog's ears, his eyes also exhibit great variation in size, shape, and position according to the breed's standard. A dog's eyeball is always round, or nearly so, with variations in the size and shape being governed by a number of factors including eyeball dimensions, eye lid development, and so forth. For example, the Australian Shepherd's almond-shaped eyes are created not by the shape of the eyeball but by the tissue and bone surrounding the eye. Some dogs, like the Pekingese or Pug, appear to have relatively large eyes, whereas the Collie's appear comparatively small. The Wire Fox Terrier's small, dark eyes are full of fire, life, and expression. The Brussels Griffon eyes are described as "almost human." Some herding dogs, such as the Border Collie, have what's called "eye"—a type of stare used for controlling or intimidating sheep. Although it's generally not aggressive, it can be downright annoying when you're eating dinner, reading, watching television, or trying to concentrate.

Friendly relaxed dogs have soft, dewy eyes that melt your heart. Dogs who want to hurt you have cold, hard eyes. Certainly you've heard the expression, "If looks could kill..." Hopefully you will never be on the end of a dog's icy, cold stare because it's usually the look he gets right before he bites. Like humans, the look is difficult to explain, but it makes your blood run cold! Throw in a head turn that points those cold, steely eyes directly into your eyes, and your best bet is to finesse the situation until he calms down.

Regardless of your dog's eye shape, size, or color, a few common denominators are present when it comes to reading a dog's eye expression.

- Direct eye contact (often showing the white of the eyes) coupled with staring usually indicates alertness and/or dominance. Can also indicate a predatory position.
- Wide open, sparkling, mischievous eyes couple with no body tension usually indicate a dog who is ready for fun—perhaps a game of fetch or a wrestling match with his canine buddies.
- Narrowed eyes coupled with ears drawn back generally indicate fear anxiety, or submissiveness.
- Squinty eyes coupled with drawn back ears, relaxed jaw, tail in half-mast usually indicate a nonconfrontational greeting.
- Wide open eyes where the whites are visible (aka Whale eye: when a dog's head and eyes aren't pointing in the same direction, so that you see the whites of a dog's eyes on one side or the other) is often seen with dogs who are fearful of strangers or other animals.

Head (Tilt)

A discussion on heads is often characterized by angles, planes, and fulcrums, and while they are super important to the history of the breed, as well as to die-hard breed enthusiasts, what you want to be most concerned with is expression. As with everything pertaining to purebred dogs, a dog's head is part and parcel of his heritage—the job for which he was originally bred. The size and shape of a dog's head can influence your perception. Consider, for example, the head of an American Staffordshire Terrier. Intimidating, right? What about the Borzoi's head? Elegant and dignified

A head tilt usually indicates curiosity.

come to mind. How you respond to a dog may be influenced by his head shape. Does the sweet, cuddly face of a Bichon Frise elicit nurturance? What about the face of a Mastiff or Rottweiler? While the size, shape, and proportions of a dog's head can influence our perceptions, his head tilt can tell you a lot about what he might be thinking.

- Head tilts generally indicate curiosity. Dogs often tilt or cock their head when trying to better hear a specific sound. (Generally, nervous dogs don't cock their head.)
- Some head tilts can be predatory, such as in terriers who head tilt just before pouncing on a varmint.
- A head tilt coupled with stiff body posture and teeth showing may indicate an attack is forthcoming, especially if this behavior is directed at another dog or person.

Head (Turn)

A head turn, which differs from a head tilt, is a calming signal. Have you ever noticed your dog turning is head away from you or another dog, which diverts a direct stare?

- A head turn can be a tiny movement or a clear and deliberate movement, with the head turning to the side and back or to the side, and with the dog holding that position for some time.
- Use a head turn yourself if your dog (or any dog) barks or growls as you approach. Diverting a direct stare will help to lessen the tension he is feeling.

Mouth

A dog's mouth is often overlooked when reading body language. Yet, whether it is open or closed is highly important to a dog's overall demeanor, with some experts noting the strikingly similar appearances between dogs with open mouths and those of happy-faced humans. Obviously, a dog isn't going to have his mouth open all the time, no matter how happy he is, but you should get in the habit of paying close attention to what his mouth is doing during different situations. You'll be amazed how much it can tell you about what he is thinking and feeling. For example, is it open or closed when he's concentrating? When a stranger approaches? When he's riding in the car? When he's on alert? When he's tussling with kids or other dogs?

- Open, relaxed mouth coupled with a wagging tail at half-mast and lack of body tension indicates joy and acceptance.
- A closed mouth may indicate stress and/or concentration, depending on the dog's body positioning.
- Lips drawn back can indicate stress and/or appeasement, depending on the overall body position and context of the situation.
- Lip licking (a dog licking another dog's lips) can be a sign of submission and/or acceptance.

The Rescued Dog Problem Solver

- Lip licking (a dog licking his own lips) can indicate stress.
- Wide-open mouth coupled with panting may indicate a physically overheated or emotionally aroused dog.

Tongue

A dog's tongue, believe it or not, can tell you a lot about what is going on in his brain. You may have captured the classic tongue flick while trying to take your dog's picture. Many dogs find a camera pointed at them stressful. Basically, the dog is saying, *"I trust you, but I'm not happy about that thing being pointed at me."*

A dog licking his own lips can indicate stress.

Tongue flicks are an important communication skill for dogs. They are social negotiations, so to speak, and owners often underestimate what will cause a dog to feel extreme social pressure and result in a tongue flick. Some tongue flicks are quick and barely detectable. Others are highly noticeable. You can try a tongue flick to calm your dogs, too, but be forewarned—your friends and family are likely to question your sanity! Here are a few of the more common causes that can trigger a tongue flick:

- Anxiety—may be coupled with a dog's body directed backward and mouth closed. (Approaching the dog or putting your face close to his will most likely result in a bite.)
- Discomfort, such as family greetings, the veterinarian's office, dog class, or too many people and too little space (i.e., everyone trying to pet the dog at the same time). Dogs who attempt to flee from the discomfort may have a lowered head, neck, and body— as if the dog were slinking away from whatever is causing the discomfort.
- Stress, such as learning a new command or another dog approaching.
- Submissiveness—indicating to another dog or person, "I see you, and I don't want any trouble."

Tail

A fascinating and interesting indicator of a dog's emotional state, the tail relays an incredible amount of information. Most people associate a dog's wagging tail as a sign of happiness, and most times that is true. When a dog does the full body wag—his entire body seems to wag uncontrollably—it's a pretty good indicator that he is happy and safe to approach. However, contrary to public opinion, a wagging tail does not always mean "happy dog!" How many times have you heard someone say mere seconds after being snapped at or bitten, "But he was wagging his tail!"? A lot of owners have been seduced by the wagging tail, but the dog's ulterior motive depends a lot on what the rest of his body is doing. One animal behaviorist compares it to a phony smile. Think about the person who smiles—the lips curl up at the corners—but his or her eyes remain cold and hard. It's hard to describe, but you know it when you see it, and it's creepy and unnerving, right? A dog's equivalent of a phony smile is when his tail is slowly moving back and forth but the rest of his body is stiff and immobile. Most often, this is not a happy dog, and you should consider the situation potentially dangerous.

Here are a few other "tell-tail" signs:

- Tail raised means he is confident
- Tail wagging usually (but not always) means he is excited
- Tail lowered or tucked between his leg means he is frightened or submissive

Yawning

Tired dogs aren't the only ones who yawn. Recognized as a calming signal, a dog uses it in multiple situations, such as at the veterinarian's office, when a person hugs or holds him too tight, or when humans are quarreling. You can use it too, when your dog is scared, stressed, worried, or at any time you want to calm him down. Go ahead, try it! No one's watching, but if they are, they'll start yawning too because they're contagious.

Barking

Many owners try to get their dogs to give up barking, often using unfair and inhumane methods. Barking is an essential part of a dog's communication system. Barking conveys different meanings. A dog protecting a car, for example, usually displays deep explosive

This rescued Nova Scotia Duck Tolling Retriever's body— ears, eyes, mouth, tail—are relaxed and lack tension.

barks that are frequently accompanied with a frantic charge toward the window. Dogs, especially small ones who are doted on by their owners, often bark to get attention. Dogs who like to be the center of attention will bark incessantly until their owner responds. And the owner always responds! Dogs also bark when they are bored, frustrated, excited, and to release energy. Pay attention to your dog's barking—the intensity, pitch, frequency—and you'll learn a lot about why he is barking.

Developing Your Skills

As previously mentioned, developing a better understanding of canine body language and what dogs are communicating will help to build a stronger human-canine bond and will help you to help your dog. Focus on when the "cue" or signal and what the dog is doing at that precise moment. Are you at home? At the park? Is he alone? Is he playing? Are other animals present? Are you angry? Is he trying to calm you? Once you get the hang of it, you'll be surprised how you instinctively start reading all dogs. With enough practice and a keen sense of hearing, you will be able to decipher your dog's unique bark even when he's in a crowd of barking dogs. Be forewarned though—it could easily become an entertaining challenge or quirky obsession!

Chapter 4
Bonding

Casey—A Relationship Built on Trust

Born a beautiful bundle of black and white and copper, Casey was the quintessential black tri Australian Shepherd. A puppy filled with boundless energy and limitless potential—maybe a future herding or agility superstar or a treasured jogging companion. Unknown circumstances landed Casey in a Colorado humane society, and owner ignorance landed him back in various shelters—three, possibly four times in his short three years of life. Like so many misunderstood dogs, Casey bounced around from shelter to shelter and owner to owner for breaking rules he didn't even know existed.

At one time Casey (formerly Dino) may have been a well-cared for and loved family pet. He knew Sit and Down, but how he ended up in a shelter the first time is anyone's guess. Perhaps his owner passed away or, as some suspect, he inadvertently became lost and was picked up as a stray and taken to a local shelter. Maybe his owner surrendered him to the shelter, unable to manage the breed's personality and temperament. Arriving at the shelter with no identification, it's impossible to say with any certainty how the black tri Aussie ended up in the system where steel gates slammed shut behind him.

Casey was adopted and returned to a different shelter before finding his way to the Foothills Animal Shelter in Golden, Colorado, where he was surrendered because he

chewed his bed and crate, and, when confined alone in a laundry room, he chewed the door and drywall. Separation anxiety was the owner's official diagnosis. An owner who was seemingly unable or unwilling to put in the time and effort learning to deal with the physical and mental requirements of a three-year-old turbo-charged breed. An owner who did not understand that

> IT WAS "LOVE AT FIRST SIGHT" FOR CASEY AND HIS RESCUE FAMILY.

isolation will drive most dogs insane. Casey's scarred gums and worn, broken teeth are a sad and unforgiving memento telling the story of a promising young dog's mismanagement.

Casey was adopted by another family—his third family in as many years—but was returned three days later. Settling into a new home is stressful for most dogs, and it can take a few days, a few weeks, or a few months. When you take an already anxious, stressed, and emotionally lost herding dog who is tossing out a zillion stress signals, mix in a thunderstorm, add inexperienced owners, and top it off with a small child who feels compelled to smother the dog with hugs—you have a recipe for disaster. The first night in his new home, so the story goes, Casey nipped the child who was trying to hug him because he was afraid of the thunder. Three days later, the "aggressive" dog once again found himself relegated to a shelter environment for failing to live up to unrealistic human expectations.

Many dogs end up in shelters because they are misunderstood. Behavioral issues, or behavioral issues that owners perceive as problematic, cost many dogs

ISOLATION DROVE CASEY TO PROBLEM CHEWING.

their lives, especially when humans give up on them. More often than not, problems arise because owners neglect to set boundaries or guidelines or provide structure when the dogs are young and most impressionable. It may be cute and funny when an eight-pound puppy nips at your pant legs, but not so funny when he's sixty-pounds of dynamite biting and shredding your pant leg.

Casey's saving grace was Troy Kerstetter, director of operations at Foothills Animal Shelter, who also owns Maty, the three-legged Australian Shepherd mix (whose story appears in Chapter 12). Kerstetter understands how living for extended periods in a shelter environment can quickly chip away at a dog's spirit. Bad behavior isn't always what it seems, and dogs living in a shelter environment are often scared, confused, lonely, and act out as a result. For this reason, a dog's true personality and temperament are often difficult to

assess. Kerstetter attributes Casey's issues with dogs his size to being housed for too long in a shelter situation with other wayward dogs. It's the *fight-or-flight* instinct, in which some dogs, depending on their temperament, personality, and history, completely shut down while others act out. For Casey, acting out and showing aggression toward other dogs became a coping mechanism. That's the theory, anyway. However, it is hard to say with absolute certainty why Casey feels threatened by dogs his size.

Sadly, dogs who are labeled as anxious, destructive, or aggressive are almost always harder to place in permanent homes. The longer they languish in shelters, the more they mentally deteriorate. It becomes a vicious circle, and adopting them into loving homes becomes harder with each passing day. Without Kerstetter's intervention, there was a high probability Casey would have perished.

Believing Casey could flourish given the right owners and not wanting him to languish and subsequently deteriorate further in a shelter setting, Kerstetter fostered the black-tri boy not knowing whether he would ever find a permanent, loving home. "He was a perfect house companion with me and learned to catch a Frisbee in the air in less than fifteen minutes," says Kerstetter. "I never worried about aggression, but I didn't want him to bounce from home to home any longer."

To The Rescue!

Having recently lost their rescue Beagle, Ken and Leah Stafford were not looking for another dog. Not yet. The heartache of losing Hanna cut too deep. Hearing about Casey and his situation, the Staffords began to think about him more and more. Could they adopt him? Could they give him the forever home he needed? Were they prepared to sacrifice for a dog whose past was sketchy and whose behaviors were less than stellar? No! They weren't experienced enough to handle a problematic dog. The timing wasn't right. They couldn't possibly take another dog. Not yet. That week, Leah made the twenty-two-hour drive from central California to Golden, Colorado. The only question remaining: Would Casey be everything they had hoped?

Love at first sight is how Leah describes their initial meeting in May 2013. "Casey was brought into the room, where I was sitting on the floor waiting to meet him," says Leah. "He buried his head in my chest and I hugged him." The gratefulness in the black-tri's eyes was unmistakable. Casey had not yet given up on humans. Okay, sure, had Leah known how challenging the first year would be, she might have jumped in her car and high-tailed it back to Yosemite without him. But she did not. Instead, she kissed his nose and promised she would always be there to take care of him, to love him, and to never give up on him. No more shelters for this lucky boy!

Rescue Tip: No Longer a Rescue

Keep in mind that your new dog stopped being a rescue the second he came to live with you. The day you adopted him—that's the first day of his new life. Avoid feeding into his phobias by continuing to call him a rescue dog or by focusing on his shortcomings. Focus on the positive and build on his strengths as you go about laying the foundation for a strong human-canine bond.

It quickly dawned on the Staffords that nothing they had learned from their previous rescue had prepared them for Casey. He barked. He chased squirrels and deer. He lunged at other dogs while on leash, and being trusted off leash was not an option. He snapped at a man at a truck stop, lunged at a man in a pet store, and nipped the Staffords' eighty-year-old neighbor—and that was just in the first week! With four confirmed snaps, if you count the hugging child, he was well on his way to being a repeat offender with an unscrupulous reputation. It seemed only a matter of time before Casey landed himself in serious trouble with only one way out.

Casey appeared afraid of unfamiliar people, and, rather than retreat like some dogs, he expressed his fear by snapping. Certainly, if he'd wanted to, he easily could have drawn blood. "I'll get you before you get me" seemed to be Casey's philosophy, which is not uncommon in fearful dogs. Was it Casey's desperate attempt to keep strangers away? Aggression? A reactive nature? A lack of early socialization?

Although it's easy to point a finger at abuse, some dogs inherit a shyness that can in part explain a fear of strangers. Either way, it was not acceptable behavior, and it was one that needed to be addressed immediately.

The Staffords had a steep learning curve, but they have done everything right to better understand and assess Casey's quirky and sometimes unexplainable and often frustrating behaviors. They provided Casey with the love, training, socialization, security, direction, guidance, and structure he needed to be the awesome dog he was born to be. They started right away managing Casey's environment, letting him know he was safe, yet drastically minimizing his opportunities to get himself into trouble. They learned about the history and origin of the Australian Shepherd breed, which helped to explain a few of his seemingly unexplainable behaviors. They read dozens of dog training and behavior books, worked with an experienced dog trainer, and attended three levels and eighteen weeks of dog training classes.

From day one, the Staffords have provided Casey with physical and mental stimulation by walking him 4–5 miles (8 km) per day, teaching him fun tricks, taking him for rides in the car and runs on the beach, and including him in every family outing and get-together. To be sure Casey could be included in every family vacation, they bought a travel trailer to counter the "No Dogs" motel dilemma. Perhaps most importantly, the Staffords' committed themselves to Casey. They continue to put the time, effort, and energy into making a better life for Casey, as well as helping him to be a good canine citizen.

With proper training, patience, and a huge commitment from his new owners, Casey is a different dog. Structure, guidance, and direction changed his life for the good. He has learned how to trust his owners and to trust change. Once fearful, his profound brilliance radiates confidence, and he's a self-thinker—in a good way. Today, he struts his stuff on the beaches and hiking trails close to his Yosemite home. Most importantly, fear no longer rules his daily interactions. He's comfortable around nearly everyone he meets and has turned from a highly reactive dog into a social butterfly, greeting people with the characteristic Aussie bum wiggle. Not yet 100 percent reliable off leash in an unsecured environment, he's getting there. He reliably comes when called under moderate distractions, which is a gigantic hurdle overcome. Yet, he remains easily stimulated by deer, squirrels, and other small critters scurrying around. (He's a herding dog. What more can you say?)

Although he is seldom left alone at home—only because his owners love taking him everywhere—he has, on rare occasions, such as when the weather is too hot, been left alone in the house with no problem. No whining. No barking. No destruction. Just the amazing dog he was born to be.

Matching Casey with the right owners drastically increased the odds that he would remain with the Staffords for his lifetime, thereby reducing his chance of being returned to the shelter. Isn't that what rescue is all about?

Interacting with your dog is a great way to build a strong human/canine bond.

Building a Relationship

Why do some rescue dogs, like Casey, flourish while others falter? Much has to do with genetics, but a huge component is the human-canine relationship. Everything about dog training and the human-canine bond comes down to the relationship you have with your dog. A relationship that starts the moment you meet. Understanding both will serve you well because your dog is counting on you to be there for him, to help him be successful, to be fair, and to be his teammate.

Have you ever noticed the love affair between some dogs and their owners? Not one of those clingy, neurotic, OCD-type relationships, but rather dogs who are oblivious to everyone and everything but their owners. Sure, you've seen them. They're the dogs who think their owners hang the moon. The dogs and owners who only have eyes for each other. Do you wish your dog swooned over you instead of dashing off to chase bugs or roll in something stinky?

What separates the swooners from their unruly counterparts is a strong human-canine bond built on a foundation of mutual love and respect.

Craving a stronger relationship with your dog is a good thing, but keep in mind that bonding takes time and work. Although it is time well spent, it doesn't necessarily develop overnight. Some owners fall in love with their dog at first sight, forming an

Love *and* bonding connect you to your dog.

immediate attachment. That's very common, but loving a dog isn't necessarily the same as sharing a strong bond. Think of it this way: you may love your in-laws, cousins, or siblings, but you are bonded with your best friend. You spend time together—laughing, goofing off, gossiping, commiserating, sharing secrets, skiing, golfing, shopping, and whatever. You relish and look forward to being together. You may love a lot of people, but you may have little in common with them, which hampers the bonding process.

Love *and* bonding connect you to your dog. You may experience different levels of bonding, too, as it's an ongoing process that requires trust—which can take time, especially for rescued dogs who have come from neglectful or abusive environments. Having more than one dog means you probably have a different relationship with each dog, and there's nothing wrong with that. We have dogs that we love, and then we have dogs that connect to us on a much deeper level. These dogs seem to read our minds and think we are the best thing since chopped liver. They become a part of us. They make life better than it ever could have been without them. Some people call these dogs "heart dogs" or "soul dogs."

Some human-canine bonds are so strong, owners choose to stay home with their dogs rather than go out for dinner or shopping or a movie. Others refuse to go on vacation if it means leaving their dogs behind. Those with little or no disposable income spend their last dollars on dog food and toys. Labeling them as crazy, foolish, senseless (or worse!) is easy, but the depth of love, devotion, and bonding people feel for their dogs is complex and not easily explained by one factor or lumped into one reason.

Consider this, too, oxytocin (the "feel good" hormone) is associated with social bonding. A small research project indicated that people whose dogs gazed at them had "significantly higher levels of oxytocin after the experiment" than those owners whose dogs looked at them for shorter periods. Of course, myriad hypotheses exist, and individuals vary in how much of the hormone they produce and utilize effectively. Without scientific data, it stands to reason that people who are strongly bonded with their dogs may have higher levels of oxytocin. Maybe it has nothing to do with science and everything to do with a dog's ability to bring out the best in people.

Why Is Bonding Important?

Owners who form a strong emotional bond with their dogs are more inclined to train them, and trained dogs are more apt to be included in family activities, such as hiking, camping, jogging, swimming, and so forth. In addition to the reciprocating human-canine friendship and all of the positives that come from such a relationship, research indicates that people who have an emotional attachment with their dogs are less likely to surrender them to a humane society or rescue organization, or give them away on Craigslist.

Building a One-on-One Relationship

Crafting a strong emotional attachment needs a strong foundation. Like building a brick wall, you set one brick in place, then another, then another—continually building upon each block until you have a finished product. Of course, when it comes to training dogs, you're never really finished. You're always building, polishing, fine-tuning, reinforcing good behaviors, and eliminating opportunities for inappropriate behaviors.

A key component is teaching your dog to bond with you rather than other dogs or toys. Sure, it sounds silly, but when a dog sees you as the

Crafting a strong emotional attachment with your dog requires a strong foundation.

dispenser of all things fun in his life, he's more inclined to want to be with you. The more he wants to be with and interact with you, the less likely he is to get into trouble. Teaching him to focus on you helps to cement your relationship and exposes your dog to new ways of problem solving. Your dog need not focus on you 24 hours a day. That's ridiculous. After all, he's a dog, not a robot. He still gets to play with his favorite toys or canine buddies and do dog stuff, such as sniffing, digging, and rolling in stinky stuff. Managing his environment helps him fundamentally to bond with you, so he sees you as the most exciting aspect of his world. If your dog is allowed to wander off and play with his favorite toy anytime his heart desires, why does he need you? If he is allowed to play with other dogs whenever he feels like it, or create his own fun whenever and wherever he wants, why does he need you? From day one, instill in him the idea, *If you focus on me, I will be so much more fun than anyone or anything in the environment, you won't even want to bother with them.*

It's an ideology that some trainers pooh-pooh, feeling it's unnecessary to be ground zero for your dog's fun. Yet, millions of dogs end up in shelters every day for being naughty, disobedient, or incorrigible, including hiking their leg on furniture, chewing, swiping food off counters, digging, fighting, running off, and not coming when called. If your dog *wants* to be with you, looks to you for direction in his everyday interactions, thinks you rule the universe, and comes when he's called, what's wrong with that? If the alternative to being discarded at a shelter is to make yourself the center of your dog's world, maybe it isn't such a ridiculous idea.

Many dogs love swimming, and it's a great way to explore your area.

Bonding Through Daily Interactions

Simple everyday tasks and positive interactions with your dog—feeding, walking, grooming, playing, exercising, snuggling, kissing, sharing your leftover cereal, and whispering sweet nothings in his ear—are great ways to facilitate and strengthen the bonding process. These small daily interactions are more valuable than any formal training session. Bonding teaches your dog that your relationship is for life and goes beyond a fifteen-minute-a-day training session. It's a 24/7 commitment.

For the first few months, keep him with you almost constantly. Before you throw up your hands and say, *"That's impossible! I work eight hours a day,"* consider that every moment spent with your dog is a learning process. You are either adding to or subtracting from the relationship you are trying to form with your dog. Plenty of opportunity exists for spending time with him and handling him at every opportunity. When you're home, spend time engaging and connecting with him, getting to know his quirky behaviors and personality, his sense of humor, what he likes and dislikes. Is he keen on tummy rubs and snuggling? Does he love asparagus? Where's his favorite spot to stretch out and daydream? Does he have a favorite trick or toy? Is he a loner? Social butterfly? Lover boy?

Depending on your dog's personality, temperament, and threshold for social interaction, take him walking in the park, hiking in the mountains, swimming in the lake, or riding in the car every day. But don't just *take* him walking, hiking, or swimming. Explore your surroundings together. Check out the trees, rocks, dirt, and grass. Smile at him when he picks up a cool stick, jumps over a downed branch, or paddles around in the water. Let your dog be a dog. Learn together how to run, slide, and swim. Take him someplace new every day, and let him know it's okay to be goofy. Let him pee on fire hydrants, roll in wet grass, traipse through puddles, and howl at the moon. Practice having fun every day, and encourage him to be a little bit naughty, in a good way.

Teach him entertaining tricks like waving, walking backward, rolling over, speaking, and high-fiving. Grab a camera and teach him to pose on tree stumps, picnic tables, playground equipment, benches, boulders, tractor tires, and whatever else you can find. Not only is it fun and interactive, it teaches problem solving, core strength, and body awareness. (Also known as proprioception in dog training circles.)

If you have other dogs, make a point of doing fun things together, but also individually for the first few months. Dog parks and coffee shops are ok, but do stuff together—just you and your dog. Take him places where he can be safe off leash, such as a fenced yard or tennis court, and let him run for the sheer joy of running. Be the first person your dog sees in the morning and the last person he sees at night. Be the person your dog falls in love with.

Having fun simultaneously builds a strong bond and teaches trust. Let him know you have his back, no matter what. Show him you will never intentionally put him in harm's way, and you will feed, groom, and train him. Let him know he's a rock star and how happy you are that he is your partner and best friend. Show him it is *you* who is privileged to be sharing this journey together, and you will love him until his last breath. Prove to him that everything you do together, be it grooming, training, swimming, walking, snuggling, or riding in the car will be fun and rewarding. Help him to be successful by always setting him up to succeed. This helps a fearful dog gain confidence and helps a bored dog burn excess physical and mental energy and feel a little more fulfilled.

Teach your dog that you are the ruler of the universe, and he'll be less likely to wander off and find something (or someone!) that is more exciting, like chasing squirrels, uprooting shrubs, or destroying every conceivable object within his reach. Developing a strong emotional attachment is the single most important thing you can do for your dog.

Communication and Respect: Essential Aspects of Bonding

Did you know the moment you saw your dog that he was the one? Like Casey, did he take away your breath as he melted into your arms? Did you laugh hysterically at the little mixed-terrier's antics? Did you think the Border Collie's stalking behavior was a riot? It's okay to admit you were charmed by these seemingly silly, goofy, mind-blowing antics. We're drawn to dogs for different reasons, and, whatever the reasons, he is and always will be the perfect dog for you.

Regardless of whether you have rescued a purebred or mixed-breed, developing a communication system that he understands is essential. Communication connects and bonds us to others, be it people or animals, and feeling connected is an integral part of any worthwhile relationship.

Training Tip: REINFORCEMENT

There's a science behind reward-based training methods. Without delving too deeply into the four quadrants of reinforcement (positive reinforcement, negative punishment, positive punishment, negative reinforcement), in basic terms, reinforcement is anything that tends to increase a behavior. Punishment is anything that tends to decrease behavior. Positive and negative don't mean "good" or "bad," but rather adding something (positive) or taking away something (negative). So positive reinforcement, the type of training found in this book, simply means adding something the dog likes (treats, play, etc.) in order to increase a behavior you want.

You must be absolutely clear when communicating with your dog.

Using Reinforcement to Communicate

Perfectly wonderful dogs end up needing to be rescued because their previous owners failed to teach them a system of learning. Luckily, it's not complicated. Reinforcement is a way to communicate with your dog because dogs do what is reinforcing to them, be it being given a tasty tidbit, chasing a squirrel, or barking incessantly. Think of reinforcement as anything that tends to increase behavior. If allowed the freedom to do so, dogs always choose what is most rewarding or reinforcing to them. For instance, chasing a cat is inherently self-rewarding for many dogs, and so are digging, chewing, barking, raiding trash cans, bolting out of doors, jumping on people, and chasing a delivery person. Remember, dogs do what reinforces them. If you reward behaviors, whether desired or undesired, the probability that they will be repeated greatly increases.

What your dog finds reinforcing will depend on his individual temperament and personality. Maybe your dog loves steak, liver, or cheese (what dog doesn't?), or maybe he's manic about a tug toy. A top agility trainer's dog loves swimming, so his reward (reinforcement) for the correct behavior is jumping in the swimming pool. Your goal is to observe your dog and find out what drives him wild, be it food or toys, or both, and to use those reinforcements to reward the behaviors you want, such as sitting, downing, coming when called, and more.

Doubly important is not making assumptions about what your dog finds rewarding. For example, some owners think that if a dog sits, and they pat the dog's head or hug him, they are reinforcing the Sit. However, if a dog dislikes head patting or hugging, he will avoid the behavior that led to the head patting or hugging, which, in this instance, is sitting. Therefore, the head patting or hugging becomes a punishment, rather than a reinforcement/reward, because the dog avoids the Sit behavior. Be smart. Observe your dog. Find out what he loves, what drives him wild with excitement, and use those reinforcements to instill and reward desired behaviors.

Communication Must Be Clear

Communication needs to be clear and tell the dog which behaviors are acceptable and which should be dropped immediately. With reactive or fearful dogs, like Casey, it's highly important to be clear, timely, and consistent in how you cue them. (In this context, a *cue* is any verbal or nonverbal signal, or a combination of the two, which tells the dog what you want, such as saying "Come" or "Get your ball." A nonverbal cue can be a hand or leg signal, a head shake, eye roll, etc., or even removing his leash, which cues him that it's okay to run around or sniff the ground.) You need to be one step ahead of reactive dogs because a nanosecond is about how long you have to manage the situation. Damage control is neither fun nor cheap! With a soft, sensitive, submissive dog, any frustration, harsh handling, lack of patience, or miscommunication can reverse your training by weeks, months, or even years.

Communication systems must be black or white. That doesn't mean nice or harsh, but rather yes or no. *Yes, that's an acceptable behavior*, here's a reward. Or, *No, that's not acceptable.* Sorry. No

Be consistent in your cue words—always say "Sit" when you want him to sit.

Rescue Tip: EMOTIONAL ATTACHMENT

Communication and respect are intertwined with bonding, with all three being essential to forming a strong emotional attachment with a dog.

reward. For example, if a dog does something you like, he gets a reward, such as a treat or praise, to let him know, *Yes! That's the behavior I want.* If you reward him with a favorite treat each and every time he comes to you, you greatly increase the odds of his repeating that particular behavior. If you repeat this routine 7,200 times for the first year he lives with you, he will view coming to you as a positive experience. This is the essence of positive reinforcement: when a dog does something you like, he instantly should get something that he likes, be it a treat, toy, game of tug, or the like so that he will want to repeat the behavior.

Without a good communication system, how will your dog understand what you want? How will he know that Come means *run to me as fast as you can right now (without stopping to sniff or pee on every bush along the way)*? Likewise, using Down when what you really mean is "*get off the couch*" is likely to confuse him. Life is less stressful for dogs if we show them what we want, and reward them for it, rather than trying to make them guess what we want.

Communication Must Be Consistent

Consistency is also paramount for communication. "Down" should mean the same thing today as it does next week and next month. Of course, the words you choose are secondary—what's important is consistency. If you choose to use the word "Here" instead of "Come"—that's ok. But be sure to use the same word every time. Using "Here" on Monday, "Come" on Tuesday, and "Get over here!" on Wednesday and Friday is likely to have your dog floundering in the gray area of confusion for weeks (or years!) to come.

Developing Your Communication System

You begin developing a communication system and building a dog's vocabulary by associating a command (e.g., Sit) with the behavior. Remember, dogs do not come preprogrammed. Repeatedly saying, "Sit. Sit. Sit! I said SIT!" does nothing to enhance your dog's vocabulary. Until you show him and reward him for the behavior you want, over and over and over again, he does not understand that "Sit" means "put your bum on the ground." So teach him a vocabulary and communication system by showing him what you want.

What is important to remember is that dogs are not intentionally belligerent or naughty. Never assume that your rescue dog has been taught basic commands. Lack of training may be why he ended up in the shelter to start with. If you are having a communication problem, go back to square one. Where did your training go awry? What do you need to do to better explain what you want? How can you better show your dog what you want from him? Are your rules and expectations, and the words you choose to use, clear and consistent?

Respect is equally important because when a dog respects you, he is more willing to see you as the leader of the pack and more inclined to do what you tell him, such as come when called. Respect stems from communication and interaction between you and your dog on a daily basis, whether you are in the kitchen, backyard, or riding in the car. Respect isn't about dominating, browbeating, bullying, or berating a dog. To have a respectful, well-behaved dog, he needs direction, structure, guidelines, and a clear and consistent set of rules to follow.

How Long Does it Take?

How much time is required for bonding? Much depends on you and your dog and how much time and energy you are willing to invest. Some people insist that only puppies are capable of bonding. Not true! Dogs at all stages of life form new bonds with humans. Consider, for example, the assistance or police dog who is often raised by a puppy-raiser, then trained by a skilled trainer, and then sent to his permanent home with a special-

needs person or police handler. These dogs are often in their second, third, or fourth home before moving to their permanent home, where they form incredible bonds with humans. Countless stories have been told of military people who have rescued stray dogs in foreign countries and formed extraordinary bonds. Casey, who had been abandoned by three, possibly four, owners, has formed a nearly unbreakable bond with the Staffords. So, clearly, bonding does not require that you start with a puppy.

Here's where genetics also come into play. A dog is a dog, right? Not quite. Dogs, like people, have different personalities, temperaments, quirks, and idiosyncrasies. Herding, working, and sporting (or gundog) breeds were originally bred to work closely with humans and, as a result, to bond with their owners quite quickly. Many of these dogs will stay with you all day off leash

Did You Know?   BOREDOM IS BAD FOR DOGS

In the absence of physical and mental stimulation, dogs quickly become bored, which leads to unwanted behaviors such as shredding furniture, digging, excessive barking, ransacking trash cans, and so forth—a very frustrating and detrimental situation for the human-canine bond.

while you weed the garden or mow the lawn. Hounds and terriers, on the other hand, are very independent. Making yourself the center of a Bull Terrier's universe may take some doing, but it is certainly not impossible and the reward is well worth the time invested.

Even within breeds, dogs are individuals, and littermate siblings can be as different as night and day. Weimaraner puppies, for example, may look identical, but they possess a high degree of variability, meaning that they will possess different temperaments, personalities, and varying degrees of instinct.

Too often, owners run amok by thinking they can change a dog's inherited traits. Temperament is a function of genetics. A dog's core temperament never changes. Many behaviors can be modified and managed, but the temperament doesn't change. Taking the sheepdog off the farm or the terrier out of a vermin-hunting environment does not squelch a dog's drive, energy, or desire to work. If you want calm and quiet, do not rescue a Siberian Husky. A Siberian Husky will never be a Basset Hound. If you want a dog who behaves like a Basset Hound, rescue a Basset Hound.

Bonding time will depend on your dog's history, temperament, and personality and his individual situation and circumstances before you rescued him. Some dogs are relatively easy to keep, despite their ghastly upbringing. They obey commands without a lot of back chatting. They don't fight with other dogs or pee from one end of the house to the other. They are considerate and don't body slam you into next week. They lie politely at your feet while you cook or watch television. Other dogs take more time and patience and require owners to think outside the box because stuffing a square peg into a round hole never works.

Like Casey, your dog may need structure, guidance, direction, and a consistent communication system, as well as an extra dose of love and patience. Many rescue dogs come with quirky and seemingly unexplainable behaviors that we never fully understand. Some dogs, because of their compromised formative years, lack the confidence and coping skills to deal with the stress associated with yet another new living environment. You may need to take things slowly, watching for signals that he is relating to you and is open to forming an attachment, such as willingness to engage, seeking to interact, and actually interacting.

Chapter 5

Barking

In the summer of 2008, a distraught woman with several sobbing children in tow walked into an animal shelter and gave up a four-month-old Labrador Retriever. Escaping an abusive relationship, the woman was entering a safe house where no dogs were allowed. Surely, the battered woman must have felt terrified and helpless, and perhaps that was somehow synonymous with the puppy who found herself in an unwelcoming and unfamiliar physical space, confined by the barred gates shutting behind her.

The young Labrador Retriever's physique was more akin to a field dog than a show dog, but where did she come from originally? A breeder? Craigslist? A neighbor? A friend? Another shelter? No one knows for certain.

What other possibilities were open to this puppy before a seemingly cursed twist of fate—an unfortunate luck of the draw—sent her to live with a dysfunctional, chaotic family who were forced to abandon her? In a perfect world, the young Lab might have gone to someone who prescribed a different destiny. Someone who might have loved and nurtured her for life. A person who would have talked to her, rubbed her tummy, rested a hand on her head, and whispered sweet nothings in her ear. A choice was made for this young puppy well before she was able to prove her loyalty and worthiness. Now the puppy, through no fault of her own, was banished—blacklisted to the shelter with an uncertain future. Yet, surrendering the puppy may well have been this woman's greatest act of kindness.

Having recently lost Preston, her competition obedience dog, Marsha Dandridge, American Kennel Club (AKC)-licensed obedience judge and dog trainer, and her husband Jim, went looking for another Australian Shepherd at the Bitterroot Humane Society in Hamilton, Montana. With no Aussies available, the young Labrador Retriever, a vision in cream fur with big soulful eyes, caught their attention. Yes, technically, Labrador Retrievers are either yellow, black, or chocolate; cream, white, golden, brown, or silver are not acceptable terms to use in identifying coat color. Yet, it wasn't the color but rather something in the puppy's demeanor that pierced Marsha's soul.

The young Lab had been living at the shelter for two weeks. "She barks all the time," said the shelter staff. She barks when prospective owners come to visit. She barks when the kennel door opens, and when it closes. She barks in the exercise yard. She barks when anyone plays with her. She barks when they won't play with her. When left alone, she barks and barks and barks. She barks when given a command to stop barking. No doubt,

all this noise pollution was a road block to adoption and a reason why so many potential owners passed her up. Interestingly, she didn't bark at the Dandridges. She simply wagged her tail and tilted her head inquisitively as if to say, *"Oh, good, you're here. I'm ready to leave anytime you are."* They say Labrador Retrievers are intelligent and intuitive. Is it possible this little gal recognized her ticket to ride?

HOPE BONDED IMMEDIATELY WITH HER NEW CANINE SIBLINGS.

Living with a turbo-charged dog requires a similar high-drive, high-energy owner, but Marsha wasn't looking for a Labrador Retriever, a breed known for its boundless energy. Ideally, Marsha rationalized, the puppy needed an active family, preferably one with kids who would run and play and burn off the breed's famous get-up-and-go and enthusiasm for life.

Leaving the young Lab behind, Marsha wrestled all night with the decision. Whatever traits the Labrador Retriever displayed that day, she eventually won over Marsha. Hurrying back to the shelter the next day, Marsha knew sharing her life with this noble creature was exactly what she wanted to do. The Dandridges adopted the charming bundle of babe with the expressive brown eyes and absolutely no training about how to be an upstanding canine citizen. Shelter life for this lucky gal was in her rear view mirror. Marsha, who named the Labrador Retriever "Hope," says, "I believed in her."

With proper training and socializing, Labrador Retrievers are astonishing family companions. It's one of the reasons they have ranked as America's top breed for more than a decade. Once home, Marsha was better able to assess Hope's temperament and personality because doing so in a shelter environment is difficult at best. Shelters are strange, noisy, and usually chaotic, and even the most stable of temperaments are affected to some degree. Hope survived the ordeal relatively unscathed. She epitomizes the breed's characteristically friendly, solid canine-citizen reputation, outgoing personality, willingness to please, and puppy-like enthusiasm that many Labs carry well into their old age. She bonded immediately with the Dandridges and her new canine siblings. Smart and eager to learn, Hope loves problem solving and is an ace at operant conditioning—firing off all sorts of behaviors to win the prize. Oh, and it turns out she does love to bark!

The barking that eluded the Dandridges at the shelter appeared shortly after they arrived home. One problem with barking is that it's contagious. Once Hope starts to bark, it triggers an ear-shattering symphony of barking from the three other dogs, and often from dogs from the entire neighborhood. Before you know it, the entire zip code is alive with yipping, yapping, and yowling.

Minimizing the stimuli that trigger the barking and managing Hope's environment help. So, too, does a boat load of patience and positive reinforcement, such as slipping Hope yummy treats in the moments she is silent. While barking at approaching visitors and running the fence line remain ongoing training challenges, the Dandridges' rescue dog with the huge heart and boundless enthusiasm for life is everything they had hoped for in a rescue. "We have never once considered giving up on her," says Marsha. "Her barking is something we minimize and manage, and the rest we live with."

Moving ahead with her obedience career, Hope has earned her beginner novice (BN) title and will compete in the open and advanced classes in the not-too-distant future. She's also training for agility, but, most importantly, Hope is a trusted, well-loved family member who makes the Dandridge home a more affectionate and entertaining place.

Why Dogs Bark

Barking is a natural canine behavior, but it drives most owners crazy and gives the rest of the canine species a bad name. Barking, be it chronic, excessive, or seemingly random spurts, is one of many reasons dogs are surrendered to animal shelters, given away, or abandoned. Although barking can be a frustrating and time consuming behavior to modify, understanding why dogs bark will go a long way in helping to prevent or at least curtail the noise.

Dogs bark for all sorts of reasons, and it's highly unlikely your dog is barking for no reason. Granted, some days it may seem like your dog is barking just to hear himself bark, and, in some instances, maybe that's true. Do dogs bark just to hear the sound of their own bark? Are some dogs, like some people, simply chattier than others? Or are dogs conveying a specific message like, "Bark! Bark! Bark! Can someone feed me, please! Or Bark! Bark! Bark! A leaf just fell in the yard"? Interestingly, little research has been done on what barking means. However, you need not have a PhD in canine behavior to know some dogs bark more than others.

A study published in 1973 on free-ranging dogs in Baltimore, spearheaded by Alan Beck, ScD, at Purdue University, showed that dogs who had owners but were allowed to roam barked boisterously on many different occasions. Yet dogs who grew up in the absence of humans and who were not tamed remained relatively quiet. Could it be that well-intended owners are inadvertently responsible for their dogs' barking? Have dogs quickly learned it is hard for owners to ignore their incessant, ear-shattering barks? Is it possible that dogs developed the ability to bark for hours on end because they've learned eventually owners pay attention?

Training Tip: Tips for Success

These tips will help enhance your chances of success in helping to deter your dog's barking:

- Positive reinforcement is much more powerful than negative reinforcement. Verbally praise and reward the behavior you want, which is your dog *not* barking.
- Dogs cannot learn an appropriate alternative to barking if you are not present to teach it.
- Dogs are individuals and learn at different rates. You may see improvement within a few days, or it may take many weeks. Remember, Rome wasn't built in a day, either!

Some barking can be traced to a lack of physical or mental exercise.

While much information about a dog's barking remains a mystery, we know that dogs bark when they get excited, when they are playing with their canine buddies, and when the doorbell rings. They bark to alert you to intruders or protect their territory. They bark when they are fearful or anxious. Some dogs bark out of boredom, loneliness, or frustration. They bark at kids, at passing cars, the mail carrier, the wind, the trees, the clouds rolling by, and a million other stimuli. They bark when it's feeding time. Some dogs bark when you play with them. Some bark when you won't play with them. Some barkers might be spoiled, anxious, fearful, or they may lack adequate socialization or obedience training.

The pitch of a dog's barking may help you decode why he is barking. For instance, some barks are high pitched: "Hey, Hey, Hey! I'm locked outside," or "Hurry, I need outside to potty!" Cluster barks are often play barks: "Throw the ball. Throw the ball. Throw the ball!" Others are low pitched: "Someone's at the door," or "Large man standing on the sidewalk." Some barks are more guttural: "Don't even think of coming closer."

A lot of barking can be traced to a lack of physical or mental exercise. High-energy breeds, such as Australian Cattle Dogs, Belgian Malinois, American Pit Bull Terriers, and Labrador Retrievers, to name a few, need daily physical and mental stimulation. Absent appropriate exercise, most dogs release their excess energy through barking, chewing, or digging. In these situations the solution might be as simple as some vigorous daily exercise, be it walking, jogging, hiking, swimming, obedience training, playing interactive games, or learning fun tricks. This also helps to improve the human-canine relationship, which is always a good thing.

Many flock-guarding dogs like Great Pyrenees, Anatolian Shepherds, Kuvasz, and Komondorok are bred to protect livestock and use their barking to discourage predators. Some breeds are simply noisier than others. Australian Shepherds and Border Collie, for example, are for the most part not noisy breeds, and excessive or chronic barking is generally not a problem. That said, when taken on a one-on-one basis, there are a number of Aussies and Border Collies who love to vocalize and backchat, and they need to be taught to stop barking on command. Shelties, on the other hand, are notorious for barking. Originally bred an as all-purpose dog who would alert farmers to intruders, their barking is part and parcel of their breeding. Many of the northern breeds, including Alaskan Huskies, Siberian Huskies, and Alaskan Malamutes, love to bark or howl. Plenty of terriers love to voice their opinion, too. Small dogs, like Chihuahuas and some terriers, often get a bad rap for being yappy. Yet no studies exist that indicate small dogs are more vocal than their large-breed counterparts.

Barking can be a complicated and multifaceted problem. Yet, for the most part, many dogs bark excessively because many well-intended owners inadvertently allow them to develop the habit of barking. For example, some owners mistakenly think dogs outgrow annoying behaviors, like barking, so they do nothing. Others think it's cute when their eight-week-old puppy barks and barks and barks, yet they get super annoyed when he is a three-year-old and still barking at anything and everything in sight. More annoying is animal control knocking on your door with a citation in hand.

Barking usually becomes problematic when a dog is too hyped up to stop barking. Yet defining excessive or problem barking is often problematic in itself. You may not find your dog's barking a problem if you're at work all day. Your neighbors, however, may take issue with it if they're the ones forced to listen to your buddy's non-stop barking. If you live on 100 acres, and your dog's barking doesn't bother you, it probably isn't a problem for anyone else. Likewise, if your dog barks at the occasional squirrel or bird in the yard, or only when a delivery person shows up, you probably don't have much to worry about.

Training Tip: Operant Conditioning: A Trial-and-Error Type of Learning

Operant conditioning capitalizes on the principle that a dog (or any animal) is likely to repeat a behavior that is reinforced. Think of it as a cause-and-effect relationship in which the dog causes a behavior, such as sitting, and is rewarded with something positive, usually a tasty tidbit. The dog quickly learns that his own behavior (e.g., sitting) causes a reward (e.g., tasty treat or favorite toy) to appear. If a dog barks and is ignored (e.g., no treats, no physical or verbal reward), the dog quickly learns that behavior (e.g., barking) pays no dividends. Dogs, at least the really smart ones, tend to drop a behavior that reaps them no reward. After all, what would be the point? Remember, dogs do what is most reinforcing. Why would a dog waste his time on something that gains him nothing?

No Quick Fix

There may not be an easy solution to problem barking. You may try one or a combination of several of the ideas below.

Prevention Is Key

Most owners of noisy dogs just want some peace and quiet. If your dog was properly socialized, he should not regard every little noise as an endless opportunity to bark. More often than not, the history of shelter/rescued dogs is unknown. Therefore, the best prevention against future barking is smart management. Preventing barking habits from developing, especially in puppies who are young and impressionable, is way easier than rehabbing a chronic offender. If your dog is not a barker, count your blessings and never put him in a position where he is encouraged to bark (unless you plan to teach barking as a trick and put a cue to it). For example, when the doorbell rings, avoid asking him, "*Who's there?*" or "*Let's go see!*" This can hype him up and encourage a quiet dog to bark. Leaving a dog unsupervised in the backyard all day can inspire him to bark at constant stimuli, like other dogs barking, a cat on the fence, birds flying overhead, neighbors coming and going, leaves falling, and life in general.

Barking at environmental stimulation is often self-rewarding for dogs. A dog barks at a delivery person and when the person leaves, the dog thinks, *"Look how clever I am! My barking made that human leave!"* Each time a dog is rewarded for barking, be it positive or negative reinforcement, intentional or inadvertent, he learns that barking works and he should do more of it.

Removing the outside dog from the stimulating environment, such as bringing him indoors and sharing some one-on-one interactive time, will help strengthen the human-

Teaching your dog to bark or speak on cue might solve an excessive barking problem.

Training Tip: KEEP IT POSITIVE

Positive reinforcement (i.e., rewarding him using yummy treats, verbal praise, or his favorite toy) remains a more productive way to deal with problem behaviors than punishment. While no-bark or electronic collars are available, they do not address the root problem, which is *why* your dog is barking. An aggressive approach that punishes your dog, especially a dog who is anxious or neurotic, will undoubtedly confuse or traumatize him more.

canine relationship and might be enough to keep your neighbors from calling animal control, again! Consider also crate training or otherwise corralling him in the house to curtail nighttime barking.

Indoor dogs are not immune from barking, either. If your dog sits on the furniture and stares out the window, like J'mee in chapter one, the outdoor environment can present a high degree of bark stimulation including neighbors, other dogs going for a walk, kids on bicycles, landscapers, delivery people, squirrels, and so forth. Consider closing the blinds or blocking his access to windows by closing off rooms or using baby gates so he isn't encouraged to bark at outside stimuli.

Take a Positive Approach

Positive reinforcement—rewarding the behavior you want, which is your dog being quiet or not barking—is a good place to start. Rather than wait until the problem gets out of control, teach your dog "no bark" by calmly praising "Good quiet" or "Good no bark" and rewarding him with a tasty tidbit when he is quiet. Some trainers like to use "That'll do" or "Enough" as a cue to be quiet, but you can use any command you like, as long as you're consistent. Think of all the situations in which you can praise and reinforce him for being quiet, such as when he is patiently waiting for dinner, riding in the car, when you are putting on his leash, when he is at the veterinarian's or groomer's, or when he sits or stands quietly at the door.

Speak on Cue

Teaching your dog to bark or speak on cue might solve the problem, too. A dog taught to bark on cue and then stop for a reward will associate the single bark with a positive reward like a yummy treat or a fun game of tug. Dogs who learn to speak or bark on command are mighty impressive, and plenty of trainers have found that when a dog

learns to speak or bark on cue, his barking decreases or stops completely. Teaching this fun "game" isn't terribly difficult, but it does require good timing—otherwise you're likely to teach the wrong association.

Start by paying attention to what makes your dog bark—someone at the door, a certain noise, the telephone ringing, another dog, whatever. Anticipate when he will bark, and, a nanosecond before he does so, say "Speak" or "Bark" or even "Yes!" to mark the behavior, and reward it with a treat. If you're using a clicker, click to "capture" the behavior at the exact moment he barks, then reward with a treat. (For more on clicker training see

For bored noisy dogs, the solution may be as simple as daily exercise.

the box at the end of this chapter.) Practice this several times a day, and it won't be long before he learns that the command Speak or Bark gives him permission to bark. You can even add a hand signal, such as holding up a finger or tapping your toe to cue the behavior.

Once you have him barking or command, make this a fabulous trick by teaching him to bark when sitting, standing, rolling over, or even how to count. Impress your friends and relatives by asking him in a happy voice, "Do you want this?" or "Say, hello!" or "Say Goodbye!" When he barks, praise and reward.

Withdraw Your Attention

Also, try to avoid shouting "NO!" at your dog. While it may seem like a good idea, in your dog's mind, negative attention is better than no attention. By yelling at him, you are inadvertently giving him what he wants, which is attention.

If your dog is barking as an attention-seeking behavior, who really knows if he's saying, *"Hey, pay attention to me!"* or *"Hey, hurry up with my dinner!"* or whether his bark means nothing in particular but simply a way to get your attention. Either way, it's best to ignore him until he quiets. For example, if your dog is barking as you fix his dinner, simply quit. Freeze until he stops barking. When he quits barking, praise with

"Good quiet" (or whatever command you choose) and continue with putting the food in the bowl or putting the bowl on the floor. If he starts barking again, stop again. Or, if he's barking in his crate to be let out, wait until he stops barking (you might want to wait a few extra seconds to reinforce the silence) and then let him out. It won't take long for him to realize that silence gets him what he wants. Again, any attention, even when given in a scolding tone, may be viewed by your dog as a reward. As soon as he quiets, calmly praise with "Good quiet. That's what mummy wants!" or "Good boy" and reward with a yummy treat.

Exercise

For bored noisy dogs, the solution may be as simple as daily exercise—a jog in the park, retrieving a Frisbee or tennis ball, or some fun hide-and-seek games coupled with any of the commercially available food-dispenser and puzzle games that stimulate a dog's brain. Many of these toys can be filled with kibble and other treats, and the dog has to manipulate the toy so the treats come out. A tired dog is more likely to sleep for several hours rather than releasing excess energy through barking.

Seek Professional Help

Exercise and obedience training are always viable solutions. However, some dogs who have developed ingrained barking habits may require more than exercise and attention. They need professional advice and they need it yesterday.

Excessive or chronic barking can be a complicated and multifactored problems that goes well beyond the scope of this chapter. However, if your precious pooch is well on the way to wearing out his welcome, your best solution may be to seek professional help.

If you go this route, do your homework and work with experienced trainers who utilize positive reinforcement. Many trainers resort to hasher methods, such as punishment, which for fearful or anxious dogs can exacerbate the situation and damage the human-canine relationship.

Using Aversives

An aversive is considered anything that deters your dog from doing something, but not all aversives are bad or punishing—even though plenty of trainers will disagree with that statement. The bigger question might be, does any aversive have a place in dog training? Depends a lot on whom you ask, and, of course, on the dog. Generally speaking, most trainers utilize positive (or purely positive) reinforcement, and that's a good thing. After all, no one wants to punish a dog. Yet, "punishment" can have completely different concepts depending on whether you are a behaviorist, trainer, or owner. While most owners, as well as many trainers, consider an aversive to be a punishment, and a punishment to be something inherently aversive that involves pain or fear, such as verbal or physical corrections (grabs, smacks, jerks, shocks, etc.)—punishment and aversive are not necessarily synonymous.

Consider this scenario: your dog gets loose and chases your neighbor's cat or horse or chickens. With a fast and direct march toward him, you say in no uncertain terms, "NO! Knock that off!" and he stops dead his tracks. The behavior stopped, and hopefully he never, ever chases other animals again. Is that an aversive? Absolutely!

Trainers committed to positive reinforcement do not recommend no-bark collars, sometimes referred to as e-collars or shock collars. Training and management are better methods for problem barking.

Would you feel badly about hollering at your dog even though you prevented a serious and potentially expensive and possibly deadly confrontation? Chances are if you occasionally raise your voice, you won't permanently damage or destroy your dog. In fact, you may save his life because most counties allow ranchers to shoot dogs who harass or kill livestock.

What about "body blocks"? Some trainers consider them aversive and never use or recommend them. Others use them to prevent a potentially dangerous situation. Would you use one to prevent your dog from charging another dog or, heaven forbid, a small child? Again, a lot depends on the dog. A hardy Golden Retriever or English Springer Spaniel might find body blocks a cool game. A sensitive Poodle or Shetland Sheepdog might be terrified or traumatized. (An example of why it's important to understand as much as possible about canine body language, to know your dog, and to be able to read him like a book.) Fearful, anxious, or timid dogs don't always react well to aversives, and they may become even more fearful or anxious, which has the potential to break down or completely destroy the dog's trust in you.

Ideally, you should always strive to be a positive trainer, to be kind and gentle, and to make training fun and rewarding for your dog. Teaching your dog rather than forcing or threatening him is always best because, too often, forceful methods backfire and exacerbate the very behaviors you are trying to solve. While dog training can be black and white, life with dogs is not. It's complicated and not easily sliced and diced into tidy categories. A zillion situations exist, and you may on occasion need to holler "Knock it off!" or "You cut that out!" in order to keep your dog from eating the neighbor's chickens, and that doesn't make you a bad owner.

Shaker Can and Spray Bottle

Shaker cans make a lot of noise, and that's what you want because the concept is that the noise from the shaker can startles the dog (wouldn't you be startled?) and interrupts his barking. Once the dog's barking is interrupted, you verbally praise, "Good quiet!" or "No bark" and reward with a yummy treat.

Shaker cans have fallen out of favor with many trainers because, like most dog training aversives, it has the potential to result in two consequences: instill fear of the person shaking the can and/or fear of noise. Plus, the effectiveness of any aversive differs between dogs. One dog may stop in his tracks at the sound of a shaker can full of coins, while another dog may not even blink. Some trainers say the shaker can concept is only effective if the can is tossed in the dog's direction (without hitting the dog). Unfortunately, most owners aren't blessed with a Sandy Koufax arm or good timing, and the entire process can wreak havoc with the human-canine relationship. Any training technique that nurtures fear and distrust rather than a mutually respectful, caring, and trusting human-canine relationship is never good.

An alternative to the shaker can is a spray bottle filled with tap water. The concept remains the same: When your dog barks, you give him a quick squirt in the face. The spray of water interrupts the dog's barking behavior. When he stops barking, praise immediately: "Good Quiet" or "No bark!" and reward with a yummy treat.

Like the shaker can, a spray bottle is an aversive training aid, and it has the potential to nurture fear and distrust. Some dogs won't care one iota about the water and may think it's a fun new game. Nervous, fearful, or anxious dogs may become even more anxious, nervous, worried, and distrustful. Neither of these techniques is recommended.

Citronella Collars

Citronella collars are a helpful and humane solution in reducing or managing excessive barking. Popular in European countries for many years, Citronella collars have been marketed in the United States since 1995. Here's how they work: A dog wears a collar that is equipped with a small canister of Citronella—a citrus oil that most dogs find distasteful. When the dog barks, he receives a brisk spritz of Citronella in front of his snout. The smell and the quick action of the mist startle the dog, which interrupts the barking behavior.

Proponents say it is a conditioned response—the dog quickly learns to associate the unpleasant smell with his barking. Equally beneficial, the dog will not view his owner as the designated punishment dispenser. Nor do owners have to worry about proper timing and whether or not they are inadvertently praising at the wrong time and thereby encouraging their dog to bark.

Experts say citronella collars are effective when the barking is reactive barking rather than anxiety barking. If, for instance, a dog is barking as a reaction to a stimulus, such as other dogs barking in the neighborhood, a Citronella collar might be helpful. When a dog's barking is anxiety related, such as separation anxiety, a Citronella collar may contribute to the problem by making the dog more anxious and, again, inadvertently create fear and distrust of you.

One Sheltie owner went to work and left the collar sitting on her counter. When she came home, her house reeked of Citronella. Obviously, it works best when the collar is on the dog!

Citronella collars are available through most pet supply stores or online vendors.

Some Barking Is Good

Ideally, your goal should not be to stifle barking entirely. After all, some barking is good, such as when a dog alerts you to potential danger or when he needs to go outside to potty. By utilizing positive reinforcement, try to find a happy medium by letting your dog know he has done his job of alerting you and now you have the situation under control.

Clicker Training: Power Up the Clicker

Clicker training is an excellent method of communicating and training your dog using positive motivation. Clicker training is based on the laws of learning and operant conditioning. It's a ton of fun, and you can transform your relationship with your dog while training almost any behavior from basic obedience commands to retrieving to clever, entertaining tricks. A clicker, which is nothing more than an inexpensive plastic device that makes a clicking noise, is a training tool that rewards or "marks" a behavior. A snapshot, so to speak, of a specific behavior you want to capture. The "click" tells the dog exactly which behavior you liked. It also tells a dog that a reward is on the way, be it a treat or a toy.

Theoretically, you don't need to use a clicker. A verbal cue or marker word such as a crisp "Yes!" or any perfectly timed one-syllable word like "Yea!" works, too. The clicker's slight advantage is that it marks the behavior in an unemotional manner.

The key is that you need *something*—a clicker or a verbal word—that marks the behavior and tells your dog that the behavior he performed is the behavior you wanted and the behavior you would like him to repeat. Without a marker (a click or verbal cue) that distinguishes a small piece of behavior, behaviors become more difficult to train. After all, absent a "marker"—how does your dog know what you liked? According to the theory of operant conditioning, reinforced (rewarded) behaviors are more likely to be repeated behaviors. Therefore, your timing must be spot-on, otherwise you are likely to mark behaviors you do not necessarily want repeated. For instance, if you are teaching your dog to sit and you click at the exact moment he paws your leg, you just told him that pawing your leg is the behavior you want. You can't then go back and scold him for pawing your leg. That's not fair. Or, if you click at the exact moment he stands up, you are telling him that standing up is the behavior you wanted. If you click at the exact moment he barks, you are teaching him to bark. Do you see the pattern?

In the beginning, until you become proficient with your timing, you may find teaching fun tricks and behaviors, such as a nose touch, spin, twist a good place to start—as opposed to jumping into obedience commands.

A number of good books are available that delve into the intricacies of clicker training. Sometimes, however, books are not enough, and you may need a trainer who can set you on the path to proper clicker training.

Getting Started

Dogs are never too old or too young to learn, and clicker training provides an avenue for building a strong bond while teaching fun tricks and useful behaviors. To get started, you need to prime or load the clicker. In other words, your dog first needs to learn that a "click" means a treat is coming. Several methods exist, and they're relatively easy to teach. Do this at home in a relatively quiet, nondistracting environment. Here's one way to "load" the clicker:

First, start with tiny treats. About 20 soft treats such as cheese, baked liver, ham, or hot dogs cut into small pieces work best, so the dog can eat them quickly. (No dried kibble or boring dog food.) You'll be doing some rapid repetitions of this exercise, and you don't want to wait 5 or 10 seconds for the dog to chew the treat between each repetition. If you're dog isn't interested, find a treat that drives him crazy!

With a clicker in one hand and a bunch of treats in the other—click and quickly (within one-half second) feed your dog a treat. Your goal is to time the click and reward (i.e., treat) closely together so the dog associates the click with the treat. Do about 20 quick repetitions. Click/treat. Wait a second: click/treat. Wait a second: click/treat. Always clicking and then treating. Remember, the goal is to teach the dog that the click means he gets a treat. If your dog hears a click immediately before he gets a treat, he will quickly learn that a click means a treat is coming. When done correctly, the dog develops an almost involuntary response to the clicker.

Click and treat 20 times in rapid succession twice a day for several days. By the end of the third day (if not sooner) your dog will associate the click with a treat, and that's exactly what you want.

Once you have powered up the clicker (sometimes referred to as *priming, loading, or conditioning* the clicker), and your dog understands the association between the click and the treat, you no longer need to reward immediately upon clicking. Of course, you still reward, but the clicker now serves as a "bridge" to mark the behavior. Ideally, you want to reward right away, but it's okay if you deliver the treat a second or two after the click.

Equally important, if you click—you must always, always, always reward (even if you clicked the wrong behavior).

Chapter 6
Housetraining

At a special place called SafeHaven Humane Society in Albany, Oregon, a five-month-old Jack Russell Terrier/Miniature Pinscher mix found her perfect owners. Queso (formerly known as Missy) was surrendered because her owners at the time felt the puppy was too destructive and impossible to housetrain. Despite a family that included several children, the little mixed-breed puppy was relegated outdoors for twelve or more hours each day.

House soiling is one of the top reasons dogs are surrendered to animal shelters, which is kind of crazy because housetraining is a relatively simple and painless process. For many owners, it may seem like they are swimming up the proverbial stream without a paddle. Yet, honestly, it is so simple—what could possibly go wrong?

Little else is known about Queso's history. Indications suggest that her first owners acquired her from a friend whose dog had an accidental litter. Yet no one knows for sure, and more than a few owners have been known to fudge the paperwork when surrendering their dog to a shelter. After all, no one wants to admit they are ill-prepared to deal with a dog.

Living outside on her own for much of her early life, it's highly likely she received little human interaction during the critical socialization stage, generally between six and sixteen weeks. Not surprisingly, shyness issues were apparent when she was surrendered. Equally perceptible, the little mixed-

QUESO HAD LITTLE SOCIALIZATION DURING HER EARLY MONTHS.

breed whose ancestry is known for its courage, intelligence, and determination spent so little time with her owners, they had no qualms about relinquishing the puppy who was never given a chance to be a good dog.

Research indicates that owners who develop a strong human-canine bond are less likely to surrender or abandon their dogs. It stands to reason that owners who abandon a puppy outside for twelve-plus hours a day put little or no effort into housetraining or building a strong human-canine relationship.

Fortunately, Queso's story has a happy ending.

When Arie van Ooyen's German Shepherd passed away, he went looking for another rescue. Knowing no dog could replace his shepherd, he decided a different breed was the best route for his broken heart. First thing at the shelter, Queso jumped into van Ooyen's arms and kissed him all over his face. That's all it took for the feisty black-and-brown puppy with the true terrier spirit to find her forever home.

Queso bonded immediately with van Ooyen and his girlfriend Katharina Koch. Initially, she displayed some shyness and timidity around men, as well as approaching strangers, yet plenty of handling, appropriate socialization, bonding, and training have brought her out of

her shell. Running, hiking, swimming, wrestling, and play-growling with van Ooyen are daily rituals. Understanding Queso's housetraining record (or lack of!), the couple immediately set up a structured life for the puppy, including crate training and a regular routine of eating and relieving herself. "She had a few accidents, which is to be expected, but she settled right in the first night," says Koch. "Since then, housetraining has never been an issue."

This feisty girl's good looks closely resemble her Min-pin ancestry. Originating in Germany, the breed, nicknamed the King of Toys, was once known as the *Reh Pinscher* (Roe Terrier) because its looks resembled a "nimble and graceful tiny deer found in the forests."

Terriers take their name from the Latin word for earth, *terra,* and their roots run deep in Britain's rural life. They have always been a dog of the common man, helping to hunt their owners' food and protect his crops and livestock from foxes and other predators.

Mix the Min-pin and terrier ancestries and you get a vigorous, alert, and spunky gal who possesses a centuries-old history as a ratter and companion. This little gal may be small, but she doesn't know it. True to the terrier traits, Queso is fearless, lively, and spirited. And can she run! She moves faster than the speed of gossip and maintains her ancestors' nimbleness. Attacking any activity with gusto and confidence, her intense focus serves her well whether she's running, hiking, swimming, fetching, obedience, trick training, or horseback riding. Spend five minutes with her, and you'll catch yourself grinning ear to ear. How fun would it be to bottle her pure happiness and zest for life and hold onto it forever?

One year after being rescued, the little dog who spent all of her time alone is a constant companion to van Ooyen and Koch, as well as to her canine sibling, Tofu, an Australian Shepherd. These days, Queso's life is bursting at the seams with love and adventure. She is wild about horseback riding and occasionally rides on the horse with Koch, but most days she burns excess energy by running alongside. With true terrier stamina, she easily covers six or more miles a day. When hiking, she carriers her own backpack to boot! When the sun sets, she snuggles up for cuddling before burrowing under the covers in a heap of sleep, no doubt dreaming about the day's excitement and her perfect life. "She has tons of personality and is definitely a lot of fun," says Koch. "She's my little cuddle buddy. I can't imagine why anyone would give her up."

Housetraining Made Easy

There's an old joke among dog trainers that goes something like this: If your dog has an accident in the house, roll up a newspaper and hit yourself over the head and say, "Bad owner! Bad! Bad! Bad!" Dogs are either housetrained or they aren't, and any accidents are your fault, not the dogs'.

Despite the horror stories you might have heard, housetraining is a relatively simple and painless process. That said, housetraining continues to cause owners a great deal of angst. To simplify the process, think of housetraining in these three easy steps:

- Set your puppy (or adult dog) up to succeed by managing his environment so he is never put in a position where he can do the wrong thing.
- Pay attention to him at all times so you can take him outside to potty, thereby teaching him that outside is where he needs to go rather than from one end of your house to the other.
- Calmly praise and reward him when he relieves himself outside.

Good planning and preparation and your unwavering commitment to the situation are the keys to success. Dogs are creatures of habit, and the housetraining process will be more successful if you spend the time teaching the appropriate behavior from day one.

More often than not, problems arise when owners complicate the matter by expecting too much from their puppy. An eight-week-old puppy is equivalent to a four- or six-month old human baby. Would you expect a young baby to control his or her bladder? Hopefully not! It is equally unfair to ask your puppy to exercise the control of an adult dog.

Training Tip: JUST THE FACTS . . .

A 2000 study published in the *Journal of Applied Animal Welfare Science* uncovers some interesting data regarding the relinquishment of dogs (and cats) to shelters.

- 88.1 percent of owners relinquishing a dog to a shelter indicated they never took the dog to obedience classes.
- 75.7 percent of owners say their dog did not know basic obedience commands when they adopted him or her.
- 91.8 percent of owners say they did not have a professional trainer train the dog.
- 91.3 percent of owners (or other family members) never received individual obedience instructions.
- 69.7 percent of the dogs had not been taught basic commands.

Owners almost always have different expectations for junior or adult dogs than they do for puppies. Everyone expects a puppy to have an accident or two in the house. It's part of puppy rearing, right? Yet, owners are shocked and upset when their adult dog has accidents. Any number of reasons exist why an adult dog might potty in the house. Obviously, anxiety, fear, or stress can cause a trained dog to forget his manners. Possibly, in his previous home he was taught to potty in a specific spot in the yard, and he may not be able to generalize from his old yard to his new one. More likely than not, he was never housetrained (i.e., always go outside, never inside), which, remember, is one of the primary reasons dogs are surrendered. Dogs who are raised in kennels or spend the majority of their time outside usually lack housetraining skills. They spent their entire lives outside, so why would they need to learn bladder control? They simply relieve themselves whenever they need to, and if you're not paying attention, it will be in your house.

Unless you know with absolute certainty that your dog is housetrained, always assume he is not and start from step one. While these methods are geared toward young puppies, they work equally well for untrained adult dogs.

Crate Training: Think Inside the Box

Before you get started, you'll need to decide which method you want to use—crate training or paper training. Sled dog racers and seasoned dog trainers often refer to a dog's crate as a box, as in "Get in your box," or "Go to your box." Crate, or box, training is by far the most efficient method of housetraining. When done properly, crate training helps to facilitate housetraining and minimize accidents. Here's how: years ago, owners did not capitalize on the fact that dogs are den animals, and they love having a place of their own in which to sleep and eat. Being den animals, they have an instinctive desire to keep their dens clean. If, for example, your dog were born in the wild, he would live in a cave or den and would venture away from that den to relieve himself. Dogs will do just about anything to avoid eliminating where they sleep. The fact that he's now domesticated does not change one iota his natural desire to keep his sleeping area (i.e., crate) clean. A crate mimics a dog's den, and, by capitalizing

Training Tip: WHY CRATE TRAIN?

Crate training is extremely useful in housetraining your dog. The concept is twofold: dogs will go to great lengths to avoid relieving themselves where they sleep. Crate training keeps the dog confined when you can't watch him like a hawk (so he isn't peeing from one end of the house to the other), and eventually/gradually he learns bladder control.

on his deep-seated cleanliness instinct, you can teach him bladder control and to eliminate outdoors.

How to Crate Train

A crate is advantageous for both dogs and humans—especially when it comes to housetraining.

Like any other training tool, a crate has the potential to be abused. It's not intended for 24-hour confinement. Your rescue should live with you and not in his crate. Doubly important, a crate should never be used as a form of punishment. It should provide your dog with a safe, secure environment. A place your dog loves. A safe, quiet place where he can retreat from other animals, rambunctious kids, and the hustle and bustle of being a dog.

Crate training your dog can make housetraining much easier.

With any luck, your rescue will be crate trained. If not, don't despair because most puppies and adult dogs quickly learn to love their crates when they are associated with good things, such as feeding, yummy treats, car rides, security, and sleep. To maximize the crate training process:

- Make the crate attractive to your dog by placing an old blanket, towel, or rug and a few of his favorite indestructible chew toys inside the crate. Remember, young puppies and plenty of older dogs love to chew, so choose toys and blankets that are safe and do not present a potential choking hazard.

- Leave the crate door open and allow your dog to explore in and around the crate. If he goes inside the crate, praise him. "Good dog!" or "Aren't you clever!" Reward him with a tasty tidbit while he is in the crate. (If you're clicker training, click and reward with a yummy treat anytime he approaches or enters the crate.)

- If your dog is reluctant to go inside, encourage him by letting him see you toss a scrumptious tidbit of food (cheese, liver, turkey, steak, etc.) inside the crate, preferably toward the back of the crate. When your dog goes inside the crate to retrieve the food, praise him. "Good boy!"

- Feed your dog his meals inside the crate, luring him inside with his food bowl. This makes the crate a positive place for him to be. In the beginning, if your dog is worried or anxious, you may need to keep the door open while he eats.

- When your dog is comfortable being inside the crate and shows no signs of stress, try closing the door for one minute. Open the door and praise him for being brave! "Look at you! You're so brave!"
- As your dog becomes more comfortable with the crate, you can gradually increase the time that he spends there. Never confine him for longer than one or two hours at a time—except at night when he is sleeping.
- If your dog whines or cries, avoid reinforcing the behavior by letting him out the crate or coddling him, such as saying, "What's the matter, baby?" Wait for him to be quiet for thirty seconds or so before opening the door (provided you are certain he does not need to relieve himself).

Rescue Tip: IT TAKES TIME . . .

Unless you are absolutely, positively, 100 percent certain your newly adopted dog is housetrained, it is always best to assume he is not. He may have received insufficient or improper training, which still makes him untrained. Dogs are either housetrained or they are not. Granted, stress, anxiety, fear, and the like can cause a trained dog to temporarily forget his manners, and accidents may occur. However, if your dog is pottying in your house, there is no shame in admitting he is not trained. 'It's highly likely that is how he ended up in the shelter to begin with because house-soiling is one of the top ten behavioral reasons dogs are surrendered. Recognizing that your rescued dog may lack sufficient potty manners will go a long way in providing a successful training plan.

Interestingly, a 2000 study on the relinquishment of pets published in the *Journal of Applied Animal Welfare Science*, which is the most current data available, notes that 50–70 percent of all dog and cat euthanasia is the result of "behavior problems." Doubly interesting, owners of "problem-behavior dogs" "(which includes housetraining issues) owned these animals less than three months prior to relinquishment.

Recognizing that housetraining can take 6–12 months (or longer!) depending on your dog's individual history, previous training (or lack of training), and other factors is a critical component in any training plan, as well as the human-canine relationship. If you are not willing to invest the time (longer than three months!) and energy into properly housetraining your dog, perhaps your life is better suited to an aquarium.

Paper training means that you teach your puppy to relieve himself on newspaper that you have spread out on the floor.

Paper Training

Paper training, on the other hand, is an older yet still utilized method of training. (So too are wee-wee pads and litter boxes.) This method works well for people with young puppies or tiny dogs or people who live in high-rise apartments and can't run down thirty floors every hour or whenever their puppy looks like he needs to do his business (although it's important not to use your lifestyle as an excuse not to housetrain your dog). After all, turning your Chihuahua or Chinese Crested into a cat is not the goal.

How to Paper Train

The concept is that you teach your puppy to relieve himself on newspaper that you have spread out on the floor. The paper is conveniently located and highly visible to the puppy, but not too close to his crate. Remember, he won't want to potty where he sleeps. Over time, you gradually reduce the section of floor covered by newspaper until your puppy is pottying on a small section of paper. Simultaneously, you begin moving the paper closer to the door. When you are home and able to supervise your puppy, you take him outside to potty. The theory being that by moving the paper closer to the door, and as he develops more bladder control, he will eventually associate pottying with going outside, rather than pottying on the paper.

The downside to paper training is that once you allow your puppy to potty indoors—even on paper—it creates the behavior of pottying in the house. Once the behavior becomes learned or ingrained, it is much, much harder to untrain. Eventually, at some point, you need to backtrack and train your puppy to relieve himself outdoors. This frequently creates housetraining issues down the road because the dog has been allowed to potty indoors. It doesn't matter that he's been pottying on paper, he's still been pottying indoors. Having a dog do his business indoors might not be a problem for the Chihuahua owner, but it's not a pretty sight when an adult German Shepherd or Boxer relieves himself in the middle of your kitchen. For small dogs, of course, litterbox training is a viable option if you do not mind having to clean litter boxes daily. This might not be a problem for the Chihuahua owner, but it's not attractive for the Great Dane owner.

Set a Schedule

Despite what your friend tells you or what you read on the Internet, puppies have little or no bladder control until they are about five or six months old. Accepting this fact of puppyhood is the first step in any successful housetraining program. Puppies mature at different rates, so your puppy's control may develop earlier or later. As he matures, he will gradually learn to hold his bladder for longer times.

As previously mentioned, you will want to follow the same protocol for adult dogs who were not adequately or properly housetrained.

Until your puppy (or adult dog) begins developing some reliable bladder control, you must take him outdoors frequently. Yes, it seems like a full-time job, but your 100 percent commitment to a regular schedule means he will learn more quickly, and that means fewer accidents in the house. And the sooner you can go back to walking barefoot in the house! The fewer accidents he has in the house, the faster he will learn to relieve himself outdoors. If you are indifferent, your dog will suffer in the long run because he will not understand the household rules.

Where owners run amok is by failing to recognize how frequently their dogs need to relieve themselves, especially small or toy breeds. Being a little breed doesn't mean they don't have to potty as frequently as their larger counterparts. As a general rule, take your puppy (or adult dog) outdoors at the following times:

Until your dog begins developing some reliable bladder control, you must take him outdoors frequently.

- First thing in the morning when he wakes up, and at least every hour throughout the day
- About 15 minutes after drinking water and 30 minutes after eating
- Immediately after waking from a nap
- Every time you arrive home
- Anytime you take him out of his crate
- Anytime he shows signs of having to go
- Last thing at night

Minimize accidents by recognizing that housetraining starts with keeping your puppy or adult dog under constant supervision. You can corral him by closing off parts of the house with baby gates, exercise pens, or other barriers or using a crate. Also, what goes in on a regular basis comes out on a regular basis, so provide your puppy with a regular schedule of eating, sleeping, and eliminating. When you are committed to a regular schedule, your puppy will learn that relieving himself occurs on schedule. This guideline is for young puppies, who, of course, are unique and individual. You may need to tweak or adjust this schedule to fit your older dog's particular needs.

Set a Plan

Now that you have an idea of when and how often your puppy will need to potty, decide whether you want him to potty in a specific spot in your yard. If so, pick a spot on day one and stick to it. Avoid confusing your puppy by moving the spot daily or weekly. This means you'll need to take your puppy outside on leash to potty so you can control where he goes and teach him "that's your spot." If you live in an apartment or condo, you may need to find a nearby grassy area. (Some people choose to use a piece of Astroturf on their deck.)

Each time your puppy needs to potty—take him to his spot. Watch him closely to be sure he relieves himself. Do not play with him at this point—just stand around and pretend to ignore him until he empties his bladder. It may take a few minutes, so be patient. Just as he is finishing doing his business, calmly praise, "Good potty" or "Good puppy."

You will need to repeat this routine many times throughout the day. Puppies are most active during the day—running, jumping, playing, exploring, and being a puppy. Because of their limited bladder size and lack of control, they need to relieve themselves many times during the day. During the night, they are pretty exhausted from the excitement and demands of being a puppy, so many puppies can sleep five to eight hours through the night without having to potty. Some puppies need to potty in the middle of the night, too. Some owners get lucky and their puppy sleeps through the night. Others are relegated to months of sleeplessness. Again, much depends on your individual puppy. Remember, your puppy is not being naughty or willfully disobedient. He is a puppy. He

Puppies are at their most active during the day.

has no bladder control. If your puppy wakes you in the middle of the night or early in the morning, it is best to get up with him. The fewer accidents he has in his crate, the less stressful the process will be, and the quicker he will learn to potty outside.

No one said raising a puppy was all fun and no work! Housetraining a puppy or adult dog is time-consuming, but the time invested at this stage will make your life easier in the long run.

What If He Doesn't Potty Outside?

If you take your puppy outdoors and he gets sidetracked playing or sniffing bugs and does not relieve himself, bring him indoors and put him in his crate for five or ten minutes, then repeat the aforementioned steps. (Another reason crate training is so efficient.) If you are not using a crate, take whatever measures are necessary, such as corralling him with baby gates, an exercise pen, or a leash so you can watch him like a hawk for those five or ten minutes so as to eliminate all opportunities to potty indoors. Do this as many times as necessary until your puppy relieves himself outdoors. Never assume your puppy has done his business. Seeing him relieve himself is important, and here's why: If your puppy gets distracted outdoors and forgets to potty (or you assume he's relieved himself but you didn't see him do it) and then you bring him back indoors and give him free run of the house—guess where he's going to potty when he's no longer distracted and has a sudden urge to go? Your carpet will be his bathroom. Curse yourself—not the puppy! If this happens, chalk it up to experience and endeavor to be more observant in the future.

If you catch your puppy in the middle of squatting in the house, interrupt him with an "Accck!" or "Eh-eh." The point is not to traumatize your puppy but merely to stop the behavior. Then immediately take him outdoors to his designated spot, then praise, "Good boy" or "Good potty."

Once your puppy or adult dog has done his business outside, then you can have him loose in the house while you play or cuddle. However, until he is 100 percent reliable, you should continue to avoid giving him free run of the house.

Teach the Come Command After Pottying

Another important reason to go with your puppy when he potties is that you can begin instilling the Come command as a fun game. When he's done pottying, calmly praise, "Good potty"—then make a game of him chasing you back to the house. Clap and cheer him on so you encourage him. When you get to the house, offer verbal praise, and reward him with a yummy tidbit of food. This works because young puppies are eager to follow you anywhere. Therefore, you're inciting a dog's natural's chase instinct. By going with him to potty and then having him chase you back to the house, you maximize every opportunity to begin instilling desired behaviors.

Adding a Verbal Cue

Even when your puppy knows to go to his designated spot and can successfully make the journey, you should still go with him. By doing so, you can begin instilling a verbal cue for the command, such as "Go pee" or "Go potty." Some owners use "Wee Wee" or "Poo poo." One notable English trainer uses the term, "Good whiz." You can choose a separate word for urinating and defecating. A word of caution: choose your words carefully. What might be cute or silly in your yard could be embarrassing or downright inappropriate in public.

Give the verbal cue each time your puppy is in the process of doing his business, so he begins to associate the cue words with the appropriate action. It won't be long before you will be able to prompt your dog to relieve himself on command, which is very helpful when the weather outside is frightful or you are traveling. No one wants to stand around at a rest area for twenty minutes waiting on a puppy to potty. Give the cue word in a calm tone of voice. If your voice is too excitable, your puppy is likely to be distracted by your excitement and forget what he is doing.

Is My Puppy Trained Yet?

The housetraining process runs amok when owners think their puppy is housetrained, but it is only wishful thinking on their part. Some puppies and adult dogs are harder to housetrain than others, and success is highly dependent on owner commitment and compliance. Chances are your puppy will not be reliably housetrained until he is at least six months old or older.

Chances are your puppy will not be reliably housetrained until he is at least six months old or older.

As previously mentioned, puppies or adult dogs who spend all or the majority of their time outdoors may take longer and be more challenging to housetrain. That's not to say these puppies and adult dogs cannot be housetrained. They can, but it may take longer and require extra diligence, commitment, and patience on your part.

Puppies between the ages of eight and ten weeks of age do not show signs of having to urinate. When they have to go, they go right away—often stopping to urinate in the middle of their play session. It is unrealistic to expect an eight-week-old puppy to stop what he is doing and tell you he needs to go outside. More often than not, your puppy will not realize he has to go until he is already going. Around ten or twelve weeks of age, a puppy will start to exhibit signs—warning signals that he is about to urinate or defecate—by circling, making crying noises, sniffing the floor, or standing by the door. Don't get overconfident and think you are home free. These are signs that your puppy is learning, not that he is fully housetrained. You mustn't become complacent. Now more than ever you need to remain diligent and stick to the program. Dogs are either housetrained or they are not. Any wavering on your part will only set up the dog for problems down the road.

When Accidents Happen

Ideally, you want to do everything possible to prevent accidents or at least keep them to a minimum. If an accident happens, resign yourself to being more observant and

Never hit or scold your dog if he has an accident.

diligent in the future. Did you miss the pre-potty signals? Did you keep to his regular feeding and pottying schedule?

Never scold or hit your puppy, and never, ever rub his nose in the mess. This is old-school thinking and has no place in any dog training program. It teaches a puppy nothing other than you are bigger and can stick his nose in poop, and it injures the relationship you are forming with your puppy. Punishing, yelling, or otherwise berating your dog will only confuse him and prolong the housetraining process. At worst, it teaches him to fear you. A puppy who lives in fear of you is likely to grow into an adult dog who is anxious and frequently worries, which can exacerbate urinating in the house and cause him to potty in less noticeable spots (such as behind furniture) as well as cause him to develop all sorts of unwanted behaviors. Instead, calmly and completely clean up the mess—using a product designed to eradicate pet stains and odors. This is doubly important if the accident is on your carpet. A thorough cleaning will prevent your puppy (or adult dog) from returning to the scene of the crime and leaving more unwanted gifts. Remember, successful housetraining is your responsibility. Set your puppy or adult dog up to succeed, and life will be much more enjoyable for you both.

Medical Issues

If your dog is pottying or defecating from one end of the house to the other, chances are he may not be housetrained. However, plenty of gastrointestinal issues may be causing your housetrained dog to have accidents, including a change in diet, such as changing foods too quickly or overfeeding. Some medications increase a dog's thirst, which can cause him to potty more often than usual. Urinary tract infections or incontinence (a leaking bladder) may cause your dog to leak or completely void his bladder. Often, these dogs don't realize they've had an accident. Separation anxiety, which is common in rescued dogs, may need to be ruled out, too, because it can be the root cause of house-soiling.

Chapter 7

Submissive Urination

As is the case with so many rescues, the dogs seem to choose the owners, although plenty of experts will scream "balderdash!" at that notion. Dogs don't make those kind of choices, they admonish. Jessica Drossin disagrees. Her search for a new rescue has plenty of quirky twists and turns that make you think some situations are too difficult to chalk up to coincidence.

Having recently lost her 50-pound (23-kg) Labrador Retriever/Chow mix rescue that she had stumbled upon behind a Los Angeles warehouse fifteen years earlier, Drossin and her family set out in search of another perfect "Lucy." First they searched rows and rows of kennels at a high-kill shelter in L.A. and then a second shelter in Burbank. "I wanted another dog like Lucy, with her funky, defective oddly angled ear, tan color, sleek coat, and sweet personality," says Drossin, a digital art photographer.

Earlier in the week, a Chihuahua-mix had been surrendered to the Burbank shelter. Her owner was moving and couldn't or wouldn't take the eight-month-old bundle of sweetness. Simple as that. With the stroke of a pen, the half-pint puppy was relegated to a shelter environment and an uncertain future.

The Drossins had not even considered a small breed—let alone a Chihuahua. Having looked at several dogs, the Drossins fell madly in love the moment they laid eyes on the bouncy, happy, friendly Chihuahua mix whose ancestors trace back to 1850 in the Mexican state of Chihuahua. Drossin was struck by the similarities to Lucy, her Lab/Chow. The little gal had

LUCY IS A FRIENDLY CHIHUAHUA-MIX.

the same tan color, slick coat, and sweet personality. A mini version of Lucy—right down to the funky ear that had a mind of its own. What are the odds?

A far cry from a 50-pound (23-kg) dog, the spunky little gal with the breed's characteristic saucy expression pulled out all the charming antics, as if to say, "I'm the one!" She ran straight to the Drossins, dancing on her hind legs, wiggling uncontrollably, and licking their hands. "She was so engaging," says Drossin. "She embraced us. We were sold."

The gate sheet contained zero information except for the little dog's name: Lucy. Another coincidence? Maybe. "It's kind of a bittersweet thing to have a new dog that shares the same name as your old dog, but she comes to her name and we decided that it would be most fair to her to keep the name she recognized," says Drossin. Hence, Lucy II.

LUCY ADORES HER ADOPTED "BROTHERS."

Lucy II had a 48-hour hold in case the owners changed their mind and wanted the dog back. A tense weekend passed until the dog became available for adoption. Feeling a teensy bit like a stalker family, the Drossins were hanging out at the shelter door thirty minutes before it opened to find out if they were the lucky owners of Lucy II.

The giddy family knew this wee south-of-the-border starlet was meant to be a part of their household from the first day they laid eyes on her, but a paper snafu nearly nixed the plan. Quickly resolved, the Drossins packed up their super-charged ball of exuberance, and Lucy II strutted off to her new home like a movie star prancing down the red carpet. With her outgoing personality, Lucy II immediately bonded with her new family and vice versa. Yet, this 13-pound (6-kg) gal who packs a good dose of willingness to please, self-reliance, and determination also has a timid, submissive side.

House-soiling remains a top reason many owners surrender their dogs to animal shelters, and Lucy II has a few issues of her own. Prime candidates for submissive urination are dogs who are also behaviorally submissive. Dogs who are physically or verbally scolded for typical puppy behaviors, such as chewing, may start offering submissive urination in anticipation of the punishment. Owners think the dog is willfully being disobedient, so they correct the dog, and a vicious circle begins.

Although the Drossins are doing everything right—avoiding direct eye contact and corrections, using calm physical and verbal body language—Lucy II's behavior remains challenging. So severe is her reaction—hiding under the bed for hours, refusing to come out of her crate, cowering at the slightest amount of direct eye contact (especially from Drossin's husband), sneaking around and pottying in corners and behind furniture—it's easy to assume she may have been badly mismanaged with inappropriate punishment or excessive control by her previous owner.

No dog is perfect. All dogs come with strengths, weaknesses, and challenges—even the blue-ribbon pedigreed dogs! DNA testing might decode some of Lucy II's heritage, but the Drossins love her for her sweet, smart, quirky, endearing personality. She loves car rides, as well as other dogs and people, and she simply adores Drossin's two boys.

Confidence building is a key part of managing submissive urination, and Lucy II is never afraid of the two boys, no matter how energetic and elaborate their behaviors. She simply joins in and goes wild—chasing them, crawling on them, and dancing on their backs. Dogs and kids, they just "get" each other. The more time she spends with them, the more confident she becomes. Her sense of fun and adventure come alive at the sight of the boys, and she simply wants to play, play, and play some more.

The Drossins are committed to Lucy II. Every day, she shows improvement and is becoming more comfortable in her new home. "I never thought I would have a Chihuahua mix but life is about valuing the things that come to you, and she was the one dog who ran to us every time at the shelter," says Drossin.

When she needed it the most, this family tossed Lucy II a life preserver, making this love story perfectly delightful. As a digital photographer, Drossin may have found her most photogenic model yet, elevating Lucy II to super model status! After all, is there anyone on the planet who wouldn't be cheered up just looking at Lucy II's amazingly goofy face and funky ears?

Not a Housetraining Problem . . .

People usually lump submissive and excitement urination in with housetraining issues, but they are different. They are behavioral issues, and whereas some behaviorists consider them to the same behavior, or at least on the same continuum of behavior, both submissive and excitement urination are involuntary behaviors, meaning the dog is not deliberately soiling in the house.

Excitement Urination

Someone once compared excitement urination to the human equivalent of, "I'm so excited, I almost peed my pants!" More commonly, it is seen in immature, young exuberant dogs. Any breed, male or female, who has not yet developed complete neuromuscular control can be affected. Most dogs outgrow the behavior as they grow and mature. In the meantime, if your dog's exuberance is causing puddles in the entryway, consider these suggestions:

- If possible, greet your dog outside. It won't reduce the excitement urination, but will reduce the amount of indoor clean-up.
- Keep your body language and tone of voice calm when greeting or interacting with your dog, and ask visitors to do the same.
- Take your dog for frequent walks so his bladder is always empty or as close to empty as possible.
- Teach your dog to relax by calmly praising and reinforcing calm behaviors, such as lying down, sitting, or standing when greeting people.
- Physically and mentally exercise your dog with fetching, hiking, swimming, and the like. Tired dogs aren't as excited as their underexercised counterparts. (Take necessary precautions when exercising and playing with young puppies.)
- Calmly ignore wet greetings, and never, ever physically or verbally scold your dog.

Submissive Urination

Most common in young puppies, junior dogs, and shy, submissive dogs or dogs who lack confidence, a dog greets his owner or a visitor by running up to them and urinating on the floor. A submissive dog also may greet a more dominant dog by piddling on the floor as he excitedly licks the dominant dog's muzzle; this is a reflexive sign that the dog recognizes and accepts the other dog's dominance. Unlike excitement urination, submissive urination frequently includes other appeasement behaviors, such as lowered body posture, flattened ears, rolling over, lip licking, or looking away.

Unfortunately, owners often read it as a behavioral disorder, a housetraining problem, or a willful act of disobedience. They mistakenly believe the dog can control himself and

The Drossins knew right away Lucy II was the dog for them. Yet, Lucy II, like many rescue dogs, probably had no idea what was happening. Reading a dog's body language will tell you a lot about what he might be thinking and feeling. No doubt Lucy II was scared, confused, and wondering why and how she ended up in a strange place with unfamiliar people. Her routine, her surroundings, everything about her life changed when she was surrendered to the shelter. Her world, her sense of stability and security were shaken and turned upside down. Even one day spent in a shelter environment can cause a dog to shut down emotionally, with some dogs going through a phase much like human depression.

The Drossins knew they were keeping Lucy II forever, but Lucy II, like many rescues, didn't know that.

Depending on your rescue's breed, history, temperament, and other factors, he may be confused, stressed, or anxious and may "act out" by pottying in the house, barking, cowering, running away, or snapping out of fear. He may or may not have obedience training, and those learned behaviors may take a backseat to his fear and anxiety. In other words, he may know Sit, Down, and Come, but his stress or fear overrides his ability to perform those commands.

Many, but certainly not all, rescue dogs need a transition period, be it a few days, weeks, or even months, during which they can learn to feel safe and trust again. Yet, too often, well-intended owners bring their adorable rescue home only to find he cowers, hides, potties on the floor, doesn't come when called, and doesn't live up to the their expectations. Often, they return the dog to the shelter, where the dog becomes even more stressed, anxious, and withdrawn, and a vicious cycle begins, one that often leads to the dog's demise.

Help your dog to succeed in his new home by recognizing he may go through a transition period. Stress, anxiety, fear, and uncertainty are common in rescue dogs. Set boundaries and guidelines, provide him with plenty of love and security, but let him know, "*Hey, we're all good. Let's just hang out here.*" Give him the time and space he needs to adjust so his positive spirit and personality can shine.

is simply urinating on purpose. Dogs don't have the mental wherewithal to sit around the house thinking, *"I think I'll pee in the house to get back at my owner."*

People often think their dogs "know" they shouldn't potty in the house. "He even looks guilty" is the most common owner rationalization. Owners go into freak-out mode and scold the dog, telling him he is a naughty, naughty boy, or, worse, hitting the dog or rubbing his nose in the mess, which only exacerbates the problem by causing the dog to become even more submissive.

In the dog's mind, he has acknowledged the owner's authority by submissively urinating. Basically, he's saying, *"I'm not a threat. No need to hurt me!"* When scolded for urinating, he becomes even more submissive in an effort to appease his owner. All the crouching and groveling (and submissive peeing!) isn't "guilt" but rather the dog waving the proverbial white flag. He's simply reading and responding to the owner's mannerisms.

Some behaviors, such as an assertive approach on the part of the owner, are more likely to trigger a puddle. Generally speaking, men, especially large, deep-voiced men, are more prone to trigger submissive urination than are soft-spoken men or women, as was the case in the earliest days of Lucy II's adoption. Fast, direct, exuberant approaches may also trigger the natural yet unwanted behavior. Interestingly, in Lucy II's case, the rambunctious, energetic behavior of the two boys revs her up rather than triggering submissive urination. Other stressors include bending over the dog, direct eye contact, and patting the dog on the top of the head.

The sooner an owner accepts that submissive urination is not a deliberate act and is one of the many ways dogs communicate, the sooner she can get on with helping to build her dog's confidence so he doesn't feel the need to piddle during greetings or interactions.

**Shy dogs often display
submissive urination.**

What to Do

Many puppies grow out of submissive urination on their own by the time they reach about one year of age, although you may see it in your rescued dog for longer periods, especially if the issue has been mismanaged with punishment or excessive control by an overbearing owner. If your dog is submissively urinating, don't despair. These suggestions, which are similar to those used for excitement urination, may prove helpful:

- If possible, greet your dog outside when you come home. Have someone let him out into a fenced area when you arrive. If no one is home, ignore the dog for the few minutes it takes for you to let him outside and then greet him.
- Greet your dog calmly, looking off to the side rather than directly at him. Move and speak slowly because rapid, excited body movements are likely to trigger urination. The fewer incidences of submissive urination, the sooner it will go away.
- Avoid leaning or hovering over your dog. Instead crouch or kneel down, keeping your upper body straight, so you're not bending over him, and you are at eye level with the dog. Scratch him under the chin rather than pat him on the head.
- Teach your puppy to sit while greeting people (first teach the behavior away from a greeting context and in a calm, nondistractive environment). Remember to calmly praise for the appropriate behavior.
- Take your dog outside to potty regularly and frequently because he has less control of a full bladder, and a full bladder makes a bigger puddle!
- When an accident happens, do not react verbally or physically. Calmly clean it up, and never yell, hit, or scold your dog.

Submissive urination is not a deliberate act on the dog's part.

Doubly important, teach him fun tricks, such as targeting (e.g., touching your hand with his nose), which, like taking a treat, encourages a more assertive, confident greeting on his part. Create situations where you build your dog's confidence by calmly praising him for doing right things rather than scolding him for doing wrong things. Catch him in the act of doing something right without having been issued a cue, such as sitting or lying down, being close to you, or coming without being called, and praise him calmly and affectionately.

Build Confidence!

Training your dog goes well beyond teaching him basic obedience commands, such as Sit, Down, and Come. Training, when done in a fun, positive manner

Follow these guidelines, and your dog will quickly learn that training and playing mean a good time with you!

- Ideally, there should not be a demarcation line between playing and training. Your dog should never think, *"playing is fun, but training is boring!"* Be silly, energetic, and creative to keep both engaging.

- Teach your dog every day. Handle him. Socialize him. Groom him. Crate and ex-pen train him. Teach him to tug, to retrieve, or roll over. Fun games and trick training are equally as productive and important as obedience training.

- Keep sessions short. Puppies have short attention spans—about 15 seconds! A nanosecond is about how long they can sit still. Stressed, anxious, or fearful dogs also need quick, fun sessions. Train three or four times a day, five or six minutes each session.

- Keep it fun! Fun maximizes your dog's focus, and focus maximizes your dog's propensity to learn.

- Choose the right time to train. Some dogs have "peak" hours, just as their humans do. Train when your dog is awake, full of energy, and eager to play. Never wake him up to train or play, and avoid training him on a full tummy or if he's feeling stressed, anxious, or fearful.

- Avoid tugging games when a puppy is teething.

- Train within your dog's physical and mental capabilities. Puppies and adult dogs learn at different rates. Progress at a speed within your dog's threshold—that area where he's still able to think without becoming bored, distracted, or frustrated. If you start to lose his attention, you might have expected too much. Or you may need to make yourself more exciting.

- Pump up his ego. Make him feel good about himself by always, always, always setting him up to succeed.

- Keep goals realistic and achievable. Doing so will keep you motivated and him eager to continue learning. Baby steps are a good thing, but remember to always praise and reward him for every correct baby step.

Teaching Sit:

Photo 1 & 2—With your dog standing, hold a treat directly in front of his nose. **Photo 3**—In one smooth, steady movement, raise it directly above your dog's nose and toward his tail (but keeping it close to his nose). His nose will follow upward and then backward, making it easier for him to drop his hind end into a sit. Once he is sitting, verbally praise "Good sit!" (or click) and reward with the treat.

that incorporates play is the perfect opportunity to help your dog transition and settle into his new home, to build confidence and bravery, to teach him to be a polite member of society, and to help build a mutually fabulous human-canine relationship.

By instilling basic obedience commands, along with plenty of play and fun games, the Drossins are helping Lucy II to build confidence. Ideally, all puppies and adult dogs should be able to perform basic commands without a lot of squabbling or back-chatting. However, if your dog is submissive, fearful, or has been handled harshly in the past, always progress at a speed that is within his limitations. Remember, training is about having fun!

Sit

Two options exist for teaching the Sit. Strict operant conditioning says you do not do anything to initiate the behavior. *Free shaping* a behavior means you click for just a little movement toward a sit, and then click for a bigger movement toward a sit, and then finally click for actually sitting. Free shaping is great but often time-consuming and frequently frustrating for owners (and dogs!) who have limited patience and just want to teach their dog to sit.

Alternatively, you can reward your dog for sitting on his own. For instance, when you are playing, strolling around the yard, or just hanging out, and he sits on his own, you tell him "Good Sit!" (or click) and reward with a yummy cookie. You praise and reward every behavior you want to reinforce, be it Sit, Down, Come, or Roll Over. This works well for some owners, especially those who are super-observant and have spot-on timing.

In the interest of expediency, another option is to lure your dog into a Sit using a treat.

A great way to have fun and build a bond with your dog while improving his confidence and your training skills is to capture a cute behavior. Watch your dog carefully and pick an action he does naturally. It could be something as simple as a head tilt or grin, or something as goofy as stretching, bowing, or rolling over.

To capture the behavior you want to train, click at the exact second that he does it and reward with a treat. It will take a few repetitions (or more) before your dog catches on and starts offering the behavior. Don't worry or get frustrated about how long it takes because this will only hamper the process. Simply wait until he offers the behavior again, then click and treat. Remember, it's supposed to be fun!

Once he begins offering the behavior, put a command to it, such as "grin" or "smile" or "bow."

If you're not using a clicker, simply "mark" the behavior you want to capture with an enthusiastic "Yesssssss!" Then reward with a treat.

1. If necessary, begin with your dog on leash (especially helpful if your puppy or adult dog has his own agenda, tends to wander off, or is easily distracted).
2. Start with your leash in one hand and a tasty tidbit in the other hand, with your dog standing in front of or close to you.
3. Hold the treat between your thumb and index finger.
4. Show your dog the treat, holding it close to and slightly above his nose.
5. As he raises his nose to take the treat, slowly move the treat in a slightly upward and backward direction toward his tail, keeping the treat directly above his nose. (If he jumps up, the treat is too high. If he walks backward, the treat is too low.)
6. When done correctly, a dog has no choice but to lower his hind end toward the ground. As his bum touches the ground, tell him, "Good Sit!" (or click) and reward with the treat. Release with "okay" or whatever word you choose to use.
7. Repeat this exercise three or four times in succession, three or four times a day.

Once your dog begins to understand the behavior, the treat quickly becomes a reward rather than a lure. Although some trainers adamantly oppose mixing training methods (i.e., luring and shaping), you are not likely to run into problems as long as you understand how to use them properly and not confuse your dog.

Down

The same options that exist for the Sit exist for the Down. You can free-shape minute behaviors that move you closer to the final Down position. You can also praise and reward your dog each and every time he lies down on his own with "Good Down!" (or click) and then reward. Or you can show him what you want by luring him into a Down.

1. Stand in front of your dog (with small dogs, it may be easier to kneel).
2. With your dog standing in front of you, hold a tasty tidbit of food in one hand.
3. Let him sniff the treat.
4. Move the treat toward the floor between his front feet.
5. When done correctly, your dog will plant his front feet and follow his body into the Down position as he follows the treat to the ground.
6. When his elbows and tummy are on the ground, calmly praise him with "Good Down" (or click) and reward with the treat.
7. Be sure your dog is in the Down position while you praise and reward, or you will be teaching the wrong association.
8. Release with a cue, such as "Okay" or "Free."
9. Repeat the exercise three or four times in succession, three or four times a day.

The Wait Game

This fun Wait game is a modified version of the more formal Stay command, but it's an ideal "game" to teach and play with young puppies, untrained adult dogs, or nervous, stressed, or anxious dogs. The Stay command is considered a static exercise, which is challenging for many dogs, especially high-drive, high-energy dogs; nervous, fearful dogs; or young puppies who can quickly become bored or anxious. Most puppies aren't mature enough to handle a formal Stay command until they are about six or seven months old (or older for some breeds). By starting the Stay command too soon, rushing the process, or overcorrecting, you run the risk of creating lifelong Stay problems by putting too much emotional pressure and stress on a young or untrained dog. Instead, begin playing a fun version of the Stay, which is the Wait command. (This "game" was adapted from an exercise used by trainer and author Bobbie Anderson.)

1. In the beginning, play in an enclosed area such as your living room or small fenced yard or patio.
2. Stand next to your dog (he can be sitting or standing) and hold his leash in either your right or left hand. (Always use a buckle collar, never a pinch or choke chain.) Have a bait bag or pocketful of tasty tidbits or his favorite toy.
3. Tell your dog in a nice, fun voice, "Wait."
4. With your free hand, toss his toy (or treat) about 5 or 6 feet (1.5 or 2 m) in front of him.
5. If he strains or jumps at the leash, which is highly probable, remind him in a nice, fun, playful voice "You have to wait! Don't you cheat!" Be proactive and try to remind him before he starts pulling or straining on the leash (or at least pulling or straining uncontrollably).

Teaching Down:

Photo 1—With your dog standing, hold a treat close to his nose in the underhand position. **Photo 2 & 3**—Encourage him to plant his front feet and fold his body into the down position by moving the treat downward and between his front feet. **Photo 4**—Keep your hand still, and your dog should fold his body into the down position. As he's in the down position, verbally praise, "Good down!" (or click), and reward with the treat while the dog is in the down position.

6. When he is standing or sitting still (i.e., waiting) nicely for a few seconds, tell him "Get it" and give him some slack in the leash. Go with him. Holding on to the leash prevents him from wandering or running off. Once he gets the treat, back up so you encourage him to come back to you (or bring the toy back, if you are using one).

7. To encourage him to bring the toy back so that you can repeat the game, put a command to it, such as "Bring it here," and tap your legs or chest to encourage him to come back. Moving backward will also help.

8. It won't take long before he realizes that bringing the toy back means he gets to continue playing.

When done properly, it won't be long before your dog thinks that waiting is a fun game. Eventually, the command morphs into stay as your puppy matures physically and mentally, or your adult dog gains more confidence and is increasingly able to hold his Wait for longer periods with low-level (and then eventually high-level) distractions.

Chapter 8

Separation
Anxiety

Serious behavioral issues plagued Bradley when Kristin Grzesek adopted him in 2011. The effects of trauma are not always visible on the surface, so when Grzesek agreed to rescue the outrageously cute and quirky Corgi mix, she had no idea how the act of kindness would change her life.

In 2010, the then four-year-old dog was sprung from a Palm Springs, California, animal shelter one day shy of being slated for euthanasia. The how's and why's—how and why he originally ended up at the shelter, how many owners he'd had previously, why he took so long to be adopted, and why no one wanted him—remains a mystery, as it often does with shelter dogs.

Fear causes a lot of problems in dogs, so it's impossible to pinpoint with absolute certainty Bradley's root cause. Did his separation anxiety (fear of being alone) result from being surrendered to a shelter, or did the separation anxiety cause him to be surrendered in the first place? Many of his teeth were rotted and loose, which may have been the result of

multiple escape attempts during his frequent meltdowns. It's difficult to say with any sureness, but it's possible someone or something robbed this little dog of everything he could have been.

Did Bradley originally come from a puppy mill? A pet store? An irresponsible owner or backyard breeder? Had he been separated from his canine mom too early in life? What role did genetics play in his fear issues? Interestingly, one might assume he received little or

**BRADLEY IS A QUIRKY
CORGI MIX.**

no socialization or classical conditioning as a youngster, and while signs of neglect and abuse are apparent, Bradley displays little timidity or shyness. He charms the pants off anyone, as long as his owner is close by.

Bradley lived a seemingly good life once adopted from the Palm Springs shelter in 2010. In retrospect, his separation anxiety issues did not appear as pronounced at that time. Most likely, constant companionship with his owner and canine sibling, Sarge, stifled his anxiety. Seven months after being rescued, however, Bradley's future, as well as Sarge's, was once again in limbo when their owner passed away.

A neighbor agreed to try and find a home for the two dogs. Possibly she understood Bradley's issues and how difficult it would be to find him a home. She positioned the two rescues as a package deal. No takers stepped forward. Plenty of people adored Sarge, but no one would commit to the crazy little red dog with the big ears and soulful brown eyes. Subsequently, the two rescues were abruptly dumped on the doorstep of the departed owner's relatives.

BRADLEY'S RESCUE FAMILY IS WORKING ON HIS SEPARATION ANXIETY.

Unable to find homes for the canine pals, and not wanting the dogs relegated yet again to a shelter environment, Grzesek, who has two other dogs, signed up for the commitment—a substantial one—agreeing to take Bradley. Sarge went to her mother.

Separation anxiety can lead to horrible behavioral problems in dogs, and Bradley is no exception. Friendly, lovable, and outgoing while within eyesight of Grzesek, yet leave him alone for even a few minutes, and he squeals, barks, and throws fits; scratches the paint on the front door; tears up stuff; and urinates and vomits in the house. The pacing and whining start as soon as Grzesek begins her preparations to leave the house for work, grocery shopping, or whatever.

Bradley's issues became evident straightaway. As soon as he came to live with Grzesek, issues began unfolding. Separation anxiety is rooted in fear, with both fear and anxiety being related behaviorally and neurochemically. At a minimum, Grzesek is Bradley's third owner, and shuffling from shelters to owners to strange homes and back to shelters no doubt exacerbated his fears. Unlike his previous owner, who spent 24/7 with the dogs,

Grzesek works eight hours a day. Bradley adores his canine siblings—a Golden Retriever and Shetland Sheepdog puppy. Yet, in Grzesek's absence, they provide little comfort or security for the dense fog of fear that envelops the endearing but anxious rescue.

Doing everything right, Grzesek followed the standard protocol of counterconditioning. She practiced predictable and nonemotional departures and greetings, left her purse in the car, left through a different door, and put on her shoes or picked up her car keys and went nowhere. Yet, because Bradley's case is so severe, progress has been minimal. As much as she tried, counterconditioning did not sever Bradley's link between being alone and feeling panicked.

Relapses are common when routines are disrupted by variations in work hours, business trips, vacations, or moving to a new home. When one of Grzesek's Shelties passed away, the tiny bits of progress evaporated, and they were back to square one. Moving from an apartment to a new home in 2014 escalated Bradley's fear, with his behavior becoming much worse. Blood work ruled out any underlying medical issues. Interestingly, the vet also ran a DNA test looking to decode any clues that might be milling about in his DNA. The "Corgi-mix" turned out to be a Chihuahua/Cavalier King Charles Spaniel mix.

Aromatherapy, herbal supplements, dog-appeasing pheromone diffusers, a Thundershirt, and obedience training—Grzesek tried them all to no avail. Even with fluoxetine, an antianxiety drug prescribed by the veterinarian, the little mixed-breed still goes into a full-scale panic attack at the mere anticipation of being left alone. The medication helps, but three years after being rescued, Bradley still needs to be corralled for his own safety when left alone.

Kristin has a love for Bradley that has carried her through the most frustrating, discouraging, and trying times, and the connection goes both ways. His eyes shine brightly, overflowing with all the gratitude and happiness in the world. If he could speak, surely he would say, "Thank you for not giving up on me."

"He's the cutest most loving little dog," says Grzesek. "He gives big kisses in the morning, and charms everyone when I take him out in public. Some days he drives me crazy, but he has the sweetest heart. He just wags his tail and he makes me want to keep working with him."

Sharing stories about Bradley's enormous heart and gentle spirit, Grzesek's love radiates for the little rescue no one wanted. What they mean to each other on a deeper level is clear, and one senses it is Grzesek who feels lucky to be a part of Bradley's journey. Recognizing that Bradley's training will never progress in a quick or straight line, Grzesek remains committed to years of training, counterconditioning, cleaning up accidents, accepting setbacks, and celebrating progress—progress that is almost always measured in baby steps. And that's okay, especially when Bradley curls up next to Grzesek for endless kisses and cuddles and calmly watches the world go by.

Many dogs suffer from separation anxiety.

Separation Anxiety

Plenty of rescue dogs are happy to curl up and hang out while you are away working, shopping, running errands, or whatever. Recognizing that you leave from time to time is part of their normal day-to-day doggie routine. Yet, many dogs suffer from separation anxiety, becoming anxious or panicked at the mere anticipation of being left alone. These dogs want nothing more than to be near you, and they literally become traumatized when left alone. Stores have been told of dogs who jumped through windows or destroyed drywall, vinyl flooring, window sills, or door frames. They potty in the house, bark, whine, or pace incessantly. Seriously affected dogs can easily do thousands of dollars worth of damage in ten or fifteen minutes.

Behavior problems are one of the leading reasons dogs are relinquished to shelters or euthanized. Interestingly, dogs from shelter environments have a slightly higher rate of separation anxiety, but experts do not know if it is caused by being surrendered, or whether the separation anxiety is what caused them to be surrendered to a shelter in the first place.

An estimated 10 million dogs (up to 17 percent of the canine population) suffer from separation anxiety, with fewer than one million receiving treatment. Other data estimate one in six dogs may suffer from separation anxiety, and roughly 70 percent of dogs diagnosed in a clinical setting with noise or storm phobias often have undiagnosed separation anxiety as well.

Evidence also suggests that dogs who are not treated will only worsen with exposure, with the rate at which they deteriorate depending a lot on the individual dogs. Many owners surrender their dogs to a shelter because they think their dogs are being naughty or intentionally misbehaving. For dogs with separation anxiety, this could not be further from the truth.

The neurological mechanisms of separation anxiety are not clearly understood. We know dogs are social animals who have a strong inherent desire to be with their human pack. Some experts theorize an underlying cause may include dogs who never learned at a young age to accept periods of being alone.

Studies indicate that it is closely linked to noise phobias, including fear of thunderstorms or fireworks, which are rooted in fear. Dogs need a certain amount of fear. It's healthy and normal and necessary because it allows them to be alert and safe by

There is a difference between destructive behavior because of boredom and true separation anxiety.

reacting to actual or perceived threats, such as retreating from an unfamiliar human or another animal or a threatening situation. Think "flight" in the flight-or-fight instinct. Some dogs are more fearful or anxious than others, and sometimes that fear, for whatever reason, manifests as separation anxiety, noise phobia, or aggression.

If any canine behavior begs for professional intervention, it is true separation anxiety issues.

Separation Anxiety or Boredom?

Dogs, like Bradley, who suffer from separation anxiety can challenge the patience of owners and trainers. Yet these dogs are not being willfully naughty or disobedient. Dogs do not act out of spite or revenge. They do not have the mental wherewithal to think, "I'm going to eat the drywall today because my owner left me home alone."

Comparing dogs who suffer from separation anxiety to dogs who are simply bored or lonely and get into mischief when left alone is like comparing apples to oranges. Just because a dog shreds pillows or magazines or potties in the house doesn't mean he has separation anxiety. Perhaps he gets into trouble because he lacks appropriate training. Maybe committing heinous acts against your personal property is a result of insufficient training. Possibly he isn't as housetrained as you think, or maybe your expectation of how long he can wait between potty trips outside is not realistic. These type of training problems (or lack of training!) are often blamed on separation anxiety issues, even though these problems can easily be managed with basic obedience training and confinement to keep the dog happy and out of trouble while he's alone.

Destruction, urinating or defecating, and barking, howling or whining are behaviors owners are most likely to complain about because they are so obvious. Few owners are likely to overlook a giant puddle or a missing door jam. And no doubt your neighbors will be, well, barking mad at your dog's chronic vocalization. Subtle behaviors that you are more likely to overlook include the dog following you everywhere, pacing, whining, or drooling when he realizes you are preparing to leave. When left alone, he may pant, drool, cry, shake, tremble, or refuse to eat. Set up a nanny cam or video camera to see what is really happening when you are away.

Recognizing the difference between separation anxiety and lack of training is an important part of treatment and management of the behavior. A truly anxious, stressed dog is not likely to be bribed or distracted by a tasty bone or any interactive toy you toss to him as you are heading out the door. His entire focus will be on the distress and anticipation he feels about you leaving. When you leave, his focus will be in the direction you were headed as you left the room.

For some dogs, the mere anticipation of the owner leaving is enough to trigger a sense of anxiousness, nervousness, hyperactivity, pacing, and so forth. Severely affected dogs

If your dog is wreaking havoc while you're away—even for brief periods of time—
here are a few tips that may help you to decipher between lack of training and true
separation anxiety.

Destruction associated with separation anxiety is usually intense, such as digging at
vinyl floors or carpets, scratching or eating door jams, drywall, windowsills, and the
like, with the damage usually being associated with escape attempts.

House-soiling associated with separation anxiety tends to occur shortly after the
owners leave—even if they are gone for short periods of time—and should be
distinguished from accidents that happen when the dog is left alone too long.

Vocalization associated with separation anxiety usually includes barking, whining, or
howling for hours on end. It differs from typical barking or vocalizing associated with a
neighbor walking by or a cat on the fence.

may injure themselves as they try to escape once the owner has left. Therefore, many
dogs simply cannot be left alone.

But what's an owner to do?

Treatment

The good news is that separation anxiety, in most cases, can be treated. Like many
behavioral issues, it is not cured, but is simply managed or controlled to a point that is
acceptable to both the dog and the owner. The bad news is, depending on the severity
of the problem, it can be a difficult and complicated behavior to manage, and the
turnaround time is not going to be overnight. It can take weeks, months, or years before
your dog is comfortable being left alone. Sadly, well-intended owners (and trainers)
frequently exacerbate the problem if they over- or underreact to the situation.

Ruling in or out any underlying physical or biological triggers provides an excellent
starting point, which your veterinarian can easily do via a good medical workup. Next,
consider hiring an experienced trainer or behaviorist who can provide a definitive
diagnosis of separation anxiety, as opposed to lack of training. He or she can develop a
training program to help teach your dog in a safe and humane manner how to learn to

relax and to accept being alone for short periods of time. If you go this route, which is highly recommended, look for experts who focus on positive motivation and humane training methods. Harsh training will only exacerbate the situation.

Treatment is multifaceted, with two of the more common treatments being behavior modification and pharmacological therapy.

Pharmacological Therapies

For many dogs, especially severely affected ones, antianxiety medications, similar to what humans take, can mean the difference between a good quality of life and one bogged down in fear, or, worse yet, a one-way ticket to the closest humane society. Before you throw up your hands and say, "No way! I'm not drugging my dog," consider that household destruction associated with separation anxiety is one of the more common reasons dogs are surrendered to shelters, abandoned, or euthanized.

Canine behavioral medications are controversial, sometimes stigmatized, and often viewed as a "cop out" or a way for owners to avoid putting in the training necessary to deal with behavioral issues. In some instances, this may be true if the behavioral medication is not used in conjunction with training/counterconditioning. Simply drugging a dog to avoid dealing with the situation is irresponsible. However, antianxiety drugs coupled with behavioral training may be enough to save your dog's life (and your

For severely affected dogs, antianxiety medications can help.

You need to find an experienced trainer or behaviorist to help with anxiety issues.

sanity!) by providing you with an alternative to surrendering him to a shelter. The longer a dog goes without treatment, the worse the neurological pathology. Over time, the act of being distressed can cause neurochemical damage, and the damaging of his neurons will make a dog more reactive, not less reactive, over time. The earlier owners intervene with medications, the better for the dog, according to Certified Canine Animal Behaviorist and separation anxiety expert Karen Overall, VMD, PhD.

A number of antianxiety, antidepressant, and mood-stabilizing medications are available for affected dogs. Like humans, dogs are incredibly individual in their responses to medications, and your veterinarian may need to change medications a few times before finding the one that works just right for your dog.

Behavior medications are not for all dogs, which is why you need to work closely with your veterinarian, as well as an experienced trainer or behaviorist. Behavioral modification can be accomplished without antianxiety drugs, but, for many dogs with severe separation anxiety, medication can help speed up the rehabilitation/counterconditioning by helping to improve trainability. Many of these drugs help to rebalance a dog's brain chemicals that are out of whack so that he can begin to relax, thereby putting him in a better frame of mind to learn.

The medications are not intended for long-term or permanent use, but rather to be used in conjunction with training. Once a dog has learned new behaviors, including how to relax, to be calm, to accept being left alone for periods of time, and so forth, the medications are gradually discontinued. If you go this route, you will need to work closely with your veterinarian to ensure your dog is getting the best treatment possible. Routine blood tests may be recommended to make certain medications are not adversely affecting your dog.

Behavior Modification

Severely affected dogs feel the need to be next to somebody (often their owners) every second of the day, and that's a problem. Think of it this way: some dogs would love to be fawned over all day, every day, but they don't *need* nonstop attention. Dogs affected with separation anxiety *need* nonstop attention. Even then, many dogs can't enjoy the attention because they are so distressed. Treatment consists not of breaking the attachment but rather in teaching the dog he doesn't need to be anxious to get attention.

Behavior modification via counterconditioning is the primary treatment for separation anxiety.

Year ago, ignoring the dog used to be familiar advice (and it still is today, but less common). Being close to someone is hugely important and the most essential detail for affected dogs. By ignoring him, you're doing nothing to help or treat his anxiety, and doing so can plummet the anxious dog into depression. Can you see how this type of training is counterproductive?

Counterconditioning

Behavior modification via counterconditioning is the primary treatment and is pretty effective in mild or moderate cases. The concept of counterconditioning is the consistent and repeated pairing of something the dog likes (e.g., chicken or liver) with a milder case of what triggers the anxiety until a positive association is made. For example, you leaving is probably preceded by putting on your shoes or picking up your car keys. Your dog associates these behaviors with your departure. Once the association has been made, your dog may react to the shoes or keys just as he does to being left alone. In other words, he becomes reactive to a stimulus that predicts something else, which in this case is your leaving.

A component of counterconditioning is to prevent him from exhibiting as many anxious behaviors (e.g., pacing, whining) as possible in a humane way by rewarding him for being calm during the rituals of getting ready to leave. Doing so, of course, requires you to learn to recognize the difference between calm and anxious behaviors. Teaching a dog to cope with being left alone is the long-term goal, but owners often go awry when they put the horse before the cart, so to speak. In severe cases, dogs must first learn to be calm before they can learn to sustain larger periods of being alone. Otherwise, owners are simply sensitizing the dog to the departure and not to being left alone. This is tricky because many dogs who are anxious or fearful will refuse food. Equally important, the process must be consistent, positive, and repeated a zillion times, or as often as it takes, for the dog to become conditioned to the stimulus that triggers the anxiety.

The goal is conditioning the dog to associate the stimulus that triggers his anxiety (e.g., you putting on your shoes, which precedes you leaving him alone) with something he loves, so his response to you putting on your shoes or picking up your car keys is, "Oh, boy! I'm going to get some chicken." You change a dog's emotional response to a stimulus or trigger from one of anxiety or fear to one of a pleasant association.

Obviously, that's behavior modification in a tiny nutshell. Many pieces of the puzzle must be perfectly timed and chained together in order for dogs to be properly and successfully counterconditioned and/or desensitized, which is why working with an experienced trainer or behaviorist is highly recommended.

How Long Can You Leave Him?

Many severely affected dogs simply cannot be left alone. Some dogs can be left alone for a few hours but fall apart if their routine is disrupted. For example, some dogs know their owner goes to work at 7 a.m. and return at 3 p.m., but if the owner gets home at 5 p.m. or changes to the night shift, the dog falls apart. Knowing your dog is crucial in developing a routine, according to Overall. Can your dog hold on for fifteen minutes? Two hours? Four hours? If you know he can hold on for two hours but not three hours, you, or someone you trust, need to show up before the three-hour time allotment to help your dog. Again, the goal is to prevent the dog from exhibiting as many signs of anxiety as

Did You Know? No Tie Outs!

Under no circumstances should a dog affected with separation anxiety be tied out in the yard because dogs who panic can inadvertently become injured or, worse, die.

possible by removing the need for or disrupting those behaviors.

Crating

Crating is controversial, with opponents and proponents on both sides of the issues. Many behaviorists adamantly oppose crating dogs when owners leave because a large percentage will panic, with the situation becoming much, much worse. Stories have been told of dogs breaking their teeth or nails, shredding cloth crates or bending wire crates when confined. Some, although not all, dogs may adapt to being crated or corralled in a room, such as the kitchen, because they find assurance with a predictable routine. Again, the

Developing a routine is crucial to helping a dog with separation anxiety.

importance of knowing your dog allows you to maximize your management options.

Some owners can take their dogs to work, which is great if that's a possibility.

Build His Confidence

Physical and mental stimulation, including obedience or trick training, swimming, hiking, or fetching, will help to build a dog's confidence. Food puzzles, food-dispensing toys, or a Kong stuffed with food may help, but many dogs are too stressed to eat. However, these types of toys may be beneficial in monitoring your dog's progress. For instance, day after day you come home and the food-stuffed toy remains untouched. One day you come home, and the food has been eaten. A big signal in the life of a dog affected with separation anxiety!

Alternative Therapies

Alternative therapies coupled with behavior modification are proving helpful in decreasing anxiety in many dogs. As always, much will depend on the severity of the problem, as well as your commitment and compliance. Here are a few of the more popular therapies.

Acupuncture

Considered Chinese in origin, acupuncture made its way to America in the 1970s. In the United States and Canada, it is not as readily accepted as it is in Asian countries, yet its popularity as a valid treatment for dogs, as well as cats, horses, and birds, is growing.

Despite small gains in public acceptance, acupuncture remains one of the more controversial alternative veterinary practices. Some opponents refer to it as "pseudoscience" because little or no scientific evidence exists that acupuncture works in animals. Again, much of the evidence is empirical—based on anecdotes and personal observations—rather than objective scientific data.

Putting the controversy aside, acupuncture is part of the holistic system known as Traditional Chinese Medicine (TCM). The original technique, which is still practiced today, involves the insertion of very fine needles into acupuncture points that are just under the skin or in muscles that have a good nerve supply. Acupuncture points are found on *meridians*, or energetic pathways, which correspond to circulatory and nervous pathways. These meridians carry the body's vital life force or energy, referred to as *qi* or *chi*. The strategic placement of needles is believed to stimulate the release of pain-relieving chemicals in the brain and spinal cord, which produces more generalized analgesia. According to the ancient Chinese, pain is a blockage of *qi* energy, and the strategic insertion of needles corrects and rebalances this flow.

Acupuncture is part of the holistic system known as Traditional Chinese Medicine.

In TCM, separation anxiety is a "blood deficiency" and "liver qi stagnation." Veterinarians report positive results using acupuncture to treat separation anxiety, especially when used in conjunction with counterconditioning.

While many veterinarians believe the traditional way is the true way of practicing acupuncture, other effective alternatives are available including:

- **Aquapuncture**, which involves the injection of tiny amounts of vitamin B_{12} solution, saline, or other therapeutic fluids at the acupuncture points

- **Electro-acupuncture**, which involves using small amounts of electricity to stimulate acupuncture points
- **Laser acupuncture** (or laser therapy), which involves low-intensity, cold laser lights to stimulate acupuncture points
- **Moxibustion**, which involves a warming herb that is used together with acupuncture in order to warm and stimulate acupuncture points

Again, the practice is controversial among veterinarians and scientists, and you will need to determine if it is right for your dog. Never attempt acupuncture at home, and always consult with your veterinarian to help you to find a certified practitioner.

Dog-Appeasing Pheromone

Another viable option, pheromone therapy has been proved highly effective when treating dogs with separation anxiety-related problems. Pheromones are naturally produced chemicals that are used to communicate between members of the same species, and they have both behavioral and physiological effects. In dogs, pheromones are secreted by superficial skin glands, anal sac glands, salivary glands, and excreted in the urine. Some pheromones, such as sex pheromones, make a female dog more attractive to males when she comes into season. Others trigger a reaction when danger is present. Still others are used by dogs to mark territory or establish hierarchy among dogs.

The pheromone of particular interest to trainers and behaviorists is the appeasing pheromone produced by mama dogs to help calm and give their puppies a sense of well-being and assurance. This natural form of dog-appeasing pheromone is secreted from the sebaceous glands between the mammary chains of lactating dogs directly after whelping so the puppies are in contact with it as they nurse.

A synthesized version of this natural pheromone is available in a household mister, collar, or spray and is proving helpful in reducing a number of canine-related stress issues including separation anxiety. Studies have reported a reduction in separation-related anxiety when using synthetic appeasing pheromones, with no significant difference in effectiveness between it and clomipramine (aka Clomicalm—an antidepressant). Another study indicates positive results with a pheromone diffuser to reduce barking in a public kennel environment.

Dog-appeasing pheromone products, be they collars, misters, or sprays, are not a magic cure-all. By themselves, they do not cure behavioral problems. They will not magically turn your fearful, stressed, skittish, anxious dog into a brave, courageous one. However, when used in conjunction with training, they can be useful tools for frustrated owners who are contemplating surrendering or giving away their pet.

Synthetic dog-appeasing pheromones have been well tested and are generally considered safe. Because they are not systemically absorbed, experts say little toxicity or side effects exist. Of course, it's an entirely different kettle of fish if your dog eats the collar or diffuser. Then your biggest concern could be intestinal blockage.

Flower Essences

Flower essences are one of the more popular homeopathic remedies available without a prescription. Distributed by various companies, with Bach Original Flower Essences® being the most recognized brand, they work in the same energy manner has homeopathic remedies do for physical ailments, but flower remedies are for the emotions. They were first prepared in the 1930s by a British physician named Dr. Edward Bach. He isolated thirty-eight flower essences with apparent healing effects,

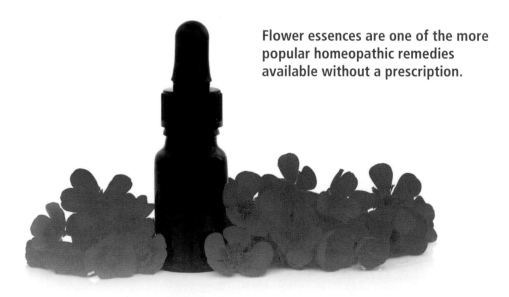

Flower essences are one of the more popular homeopathic remedies available without a prescription.

which he believed would remedy the negative states of mind. Like other homeopathic practitioners, Bach believed in mind-body medicine and that the mental and emotional states of mind played an enormous part in the recovery of illness. Diseases of the body were caused by imbalances in the body and spirit. While it's easy to confuse flower essences with other herbal remedies, there are significant differences. Flower essences and herbal remedies share a history of nature's purest ingredients. They also work with, rather than suppress, the healing process. But flower essences differ from other herbal remedies in that herbal products are made from many parts of a plant including the root, stem, leaves, fruit, seed, and blossom. Whereas herbal remedies are made using a number of methods including infusion, decoction, and tincture, flower essences begin with an infusion in water and use only the freshest blossoms of the plant. After a specific amount of infusion time, these remedies become diluted remedies and are preserved in either alcohol (grape brandy) or nonalcoholic glycerin. The majority of flower essences are sold in a liquid form that can be rubbed on a dog's gums or paws or dispensed with an eyedropper placed directly on the tongue. Alternatively, several drops can be added to the dog's drinking water.

Although flower essences are used to treat a variety of canine-related issues, some of the more common ailments include stress, behavioral or emotional issues, allergies, aggression, trauma, bruising, insect bites, and toxic exposure or ingestion. Here are a few examples and their uses:

- **Aspen** helps to ease fear and anxiety.
- **Cherry Plum** helps to remedy uncontrolled behavior or compulsiveness and helps restore control.
- **Honeysuckle** helps to remedy homesickness and an inability to cope with present conditions and helps dogs adjust to present circumstances.
- **Impatiens**, ironically, remedies impatience and irritability and restores patience.
- **Mimulus** helps overcome fear.
- **Star of Bethlehem** helps to soothe grief.
- **Sweet Chestnut** remedies extreme mental and physical distress and restores endurance.
- **White Chestnut** remedies restlessness and preoccupation and restores the ability to rest.
- **Bach's Rescue Remedy**, which combines Star of Bethlehem, clematis, rock rose, impatiens, and cherry plum, is possibly the most widely recognized over-the-counter remedy. It is frequently recommended in any situation where a pet feels grief (the loss of a canine sibling or owner), anxiety, stress, or fear, such as going to a new home, to the veterinarian's or groomers, or during thunderstorms or fireworks.

Essential Oils

While the use of essential oils for canines may not be as commonplace as some of the other natural techniques, they have been used for the health and well-being of people for centuries. As people become more aware of the healing benefits of essential oils—spiritually, energetically, psychologically, physically—it's no wonder owners and veterinarians are interested in using them for their dogs' emotional, cognitive, and physical well-being, too.

Essential oils are found in the roots, stems, leaves, flowers, and seeds of plants. These naturally occurring oils are extracted by distillation. Unlike herbal and homeopathic remedies that are used internally and externally, most essential oils are not consumed, but generally used topically or in a diffuser. Depending on your rescue dog's physical and emotional state, you may find one or more of these common essential oils helpful:

- **Chamomile** helps to calm the mind and body.
- **Calendula** in an oil form helps heal wounds.
- **Catnip** is an excellent pest repellent.
- **Chamomile** helps to calm the mind and body.
- **Eucalyptus** has antibacterial, anti-inflammatory, and antifungal qualities to help skin irritations heal.
- **Lavender** has been used for therapeutic purposes for thousands of years. It's a great analgesic and helps sooth itchy skin. It also helps to calm. (Think lavender-infused oils, shampoos, and soaps.) Note: **lavender** can be toxic to cats so always be careful when using it if you have both dogs and cats.
- **Myrrh** has anti-inflammatory properties and decreases scar tissue as the skin heals.
- **Tea tree oil** is excellent for helping cuts, scrapes, abrasions, and wounds to heal. (Commercial sprays and oils are available at most feed and farm outlets or online.)

Did You Know? SAFETY FIRST

Although essential oils are useful and generally safe, they can cause a wide variety of adverse effects. Most problems arise from the use of poor-quality or synthetic-grade oils, contaminants, or sometimes owner misuse. Animals metabolize and react differently to essential oils. Therefore, you should only use therapeutic-grade oils from reputable companies. Always consult your veterinarian or work with an experienced holistic veterinarian to minimize side effects while maximizing results.

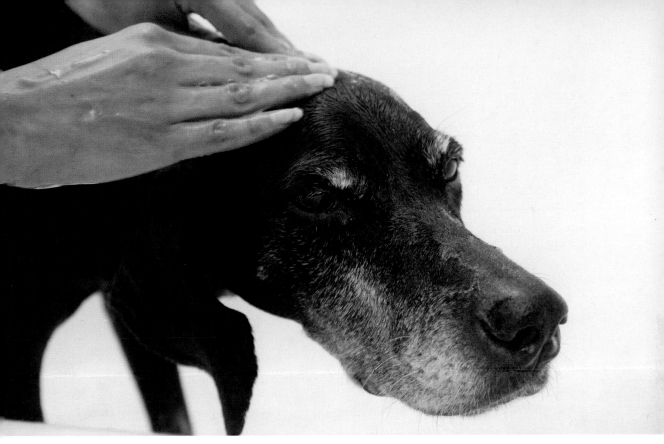

Essential oils are used topically.

- **Ylang Ylang** is used in humans for its ability to slow down rapid breathing and heart rates. It's also used as an antidepressant and sedative and has calming and mood uplifting properties.

The quality of essential oils used is, well, *essential* to success. The oils are highly concentrated, and it takes a lot of plants to fill a 1-ounce bottle. Therefore, a five-dollar bottle from the corner market probably doesn't contain a high-quality essential oil.

Aromatherapy

Have you ever crushed lavender flowers in your hand and savored the scent? What about the crushed leaves of a mint plant? No? Surely you have smelled cookies baking in the oven. Does the aroma bring back childhood memories? Baking cookies may not be aromatherapy in a traditional sense, but the concept is similar in that scents have the ability to evoke memories, set a mood, and even help one heal.

Dogs are extremely scent driven, and everyone knows their olfactory skills are far superior to ours. And aromatherapy is all about scent. Although aromatherapy is the practice of using essential oils distilled from various plants for their fragrances, who's

Plenty of alternative therapies are available for nervous or anxious dogs affected by separation anxiety. Although many owners have had good luck with these, do your research so you are not giving your dog anything that might cause an allergic or life-threatening reaction.

to know if it works the same for dogs as it does for people? Does lavender smell the same to dogs as it does to us? How do we know it's not offensive? It seems that dogs perceive scents differently than do humans. After all, they like rotting garbage and stinky horse manure. Do scents heal, calm, or invigorate dogs as they do some people? Anecdotal evidence suggests they do, but no scientific data exist (yet!)

Some theorize that certain aromatherapy substances, such as lavender, have a calming effect on owners, which, in turn, may indirectly calm their dogs. Consider that some veterinary clinics now use an electric aromatic diffuser in their waiting and examination rooms to help provide a calming and relaxing effect on their clients and canines.

Even though the evidence is completely anecdotal and empirical, if controlling your aromatic environment makes you feel better, it's bound to improve the human-canine relationship.

Herbal Remedies

Many owners have personal experience with herbal remedies, which is what started them thinking herbal medicine for their dogs. As mentioned, herbal remedies differ from flower essences, but they remain an important part of alternative medicine. Herbal medicine focuses on using plants and other natural ingredients to enhance well-being. They emphasize therapies that are designed to optimize systems' functions and correct immune, digestive, and metabolic deficiencies. Traditional herbal remedies are based on standard formulas created thousands of years ago, which reportedly have antibiotic, antifungal, and even anticancer properties. Proponents believe that prescribing whole plants provides both synergistic and safety advantages.

A few of the more common—and not so common—herbal remedies include:

- **Aloe Vera** is used primarily to reduce inflammation and heal wounds. (Who hasn't rubbed the natural gel from an aloe vera leaf on a burn or scrape?)
- **Calendula** petals applied as a paste help to heal wounds, reduce inflammation, and promote the growth of healthy new tissue. As a tea, it can be used as a wound flush.

Mixed with **comfrey** to form a balm, it can help to soothe dry, sore, scaly skin.

- **Chamomile** is one of the most common herbal remedies. Wonderful for the digestive system, it also has a calming effect on irritable or whiny dogs. (You've probably had chamomile tea to calm your own nerves.)
- **Dandelions** stimulate digestion and are good for reducing inflammation.
- **Echinacea** is known for its ability to stimulate the immune system, which helps attack foreign invaders and fight infection. (Plenty of people drink it as a tea to ward off colds and flu.) In a tea, tincture, or capsule, it can be applied to a dog's wounds, such as a dog bite.
- **Milk Thistle** helps to protect against liver damage. While it's not likely to calm your anxious dog, this important extract may help if your dog has been on medications or ingested toxins that adversely affect the liver.
- **St. John's Wort** is often called the "herbal Prozac" because it has been used to ease depression and calm nervous animals.
- **Peppermint** is soothing to the digestive tract and helps to control nausea and vomiting.
- **Slippery Elm** helps to calm gastrointestinal issues, including colitis and diarrhea.
- **Valerian Root** has been shown to have a sedative effect on animals including calming nerves, relaxing the body, and possibly allowing nervous dogs to fall asleep.

Hundreds of plants are available for use in herbal remedies, and many can be combined, such as chamomile and echinacea. How you use them—fresh, dried, in teas or tinctures—depends on the plant and your dog. You can grow herbs and plants in your garden or buy commercial products. Herbal remedies provide a wonderful opportunity for owners looking for alternatives to synthetic medications. They may even help you to save a few dollars on veterinary visits. A word of caution, though: Many herbs and plants are toxic to pets, and they may interact with conventional medications. Use any herbal treatment cautiously, and be sure to consult with your veterinarian.

Chapter 9

Aggression

Levi—A Life Saved with Love

How wonderful the life that is filled with an endless supply of toys, scrumptious food, and tender hands. Life wasn't always so grand for Levi, a four-year-old red bi Australian Shepherd who suffered the cruelest of fates—betrayal at the hands of those entrusted with his care.

Little is known about his history, from where he originally came, or how at eighteen months of age he ended up as a repeat offender, with the more serious array of misdemeanors being biting. What happened to this promising young dog is anyone's guess, but it seems apparent he suffered callous handling by humans. Levi personifies the adverse effects of harsh, outdated training methods. With biting on his record, finding a suitable home was nearly impossible. No one wanted a confirmed biter, no matter how handsome or intelligent the dog.

But in this case, Levi caught a lucky break.

Social media would save the day and give Levi the chance he needed. Modern technology sent Levi's picture whizzing through cyberspace, eventually showing up on Sandy Seward's computer. Lying alone in a snowbound Colorado animal shelter, his soulful, pleading eyes pierced her heart. Seward, a Homeland Security Customs Border Protection Agriculture Specialist and K9 Handler with a soft spot for red dogs, hit delete when she saw the post. No way could she take another dog. She already had five dogs—four of them rescues. Levi's stunning face and gorgeous amber eyes haunted her for days. She'd never met him, but she had fallen in love with his sweet face and his sad history. Unable to delete Levi's image from her mind (or heart!), Seward began the process of bringing the strikingly handsome yet spiritually broken dog home.

In March 2012, after exhausting all other possible means of transportation, Levi was loaded on a

LEVI IS AN AUSTRALIAN SHEPHERD WHO WAS SUBJECTED TO CRUEL TRAINING METHODS.

commercial flight for the 1,500 mile (2,400 km) journey from Denver, Colorado, to Fayetteville, Georgia. His fourth and final home.

Levi looks like a normal dog, but if he were a human, he'd be labeled criminally insane. His aggression issues were worse than Seward anticipated. From day one, his actions revealed the possibility of a harsh past. Seward touched his head. He growled. The type of growl that comes from deep down in a dog's belly. A growl that says, "I'm not fooling around!" Gently putting her hand in his buckle collar, he hurled himself through the air, landing in a defensive position with all forty-two teeth bared—a portrait of extreme fear. She touched his face. He growled. She touched his hind end. He flipped around, snarling and growling. Levi was living a life in defense drive. How had he arrived at this anguish? "Levi taught me things that I only imagined to be true," says Seward. "He had been manhandled and harshly trained and corrected."

Working backward in time, Levi, at eighteen months old, was an intact male taking his third plunge into a shelter environment. His history before then is unknown. Where did he come from? Why did three unrelated owners abandon him? The assumption that abuse is the root cause of his behavior is understandable. Had he been set up, framed? Was he ruthlessly handled by his first

LEVI CAN NOW SUCCESSFULLY COMPETE IN MANY AMERICAN KENNEL CLUB EVENTS.

owner? Maybe his second owner? No one knows for certain. Levi needed an experienced, compassionate dog owner. Sadly, his third family wasn't it. They were ill prepared to deal with his behavioral issues, and the promise of a forever home was doomed for failure before the ink dried on the adoption papers. Rumor has it the family's small child pounced on Levi while he was sleeping. No surprise, Levi nipped. Unsupervised rough-housing with Levi led to a nip on another child's heel. Australian Shepherds and other herding breeds are stimulated by movement. Nipping the feet and legs of fleeing children is part and parcel of the breed. Is it acceptable? No. Is it to be expected? Absolutely.

How did a good dog go so wayward? A once gentle, promising spirit seemingly broken by careless humans who mistakenly believed harsh handling and old-style pop-and-jerk type training would produce results. It did, but it nearly cost the young dog his life. It's easier to think Levi's owners were ignorant of humane, positive training methods because the alternative is to know someone intentionally hurt Levi in the name of dog training.

"Somber" is how Seward describes Levi upon his arrival in Georgia. "He could have cared less about meeting me. I believe in my heart of hearts that rather than reward him for good behaviors, his previous owners set him up to fail so they could correct him."

One day, while Levi was sitting, Seward leaned over him. In a nanosecond, his demeanor changed from docile to unhinged. Pulling back his lips, shooting out his curled tongue, with every tooth on display, Levi reacted defensively, again. "Levi is okay if you lean over him while he's standing or lying down," explains Seward, "but sitting is an entirely different matter." Other issues plagued Levi, including issues with having his head, ears, nose, mouth, teeth, or eyes touched. Aussies have a characteristic grin in which they pull their lips back and expose their teeth. A common behavior, it's often mistaken by misinformed owners as aggression. Seward suspects Levi was harshly corrected for this natural behavior.

Although many trainers suggested Levi be put in his place by dominating him, controlling him, and showing him who is boss, Seward opted for a gentler approach. Levi had been manhandled enough. Providing rules, guidelines, and boundaries, Seward set about reconditioning him with classical conditioning (using positive associations to change how a dog responds to things in his life). She retrained him to relax, control his own emotions, and to associate human hands with pleasant and safe interactions. Using a clicker, Seward introduced operant conditioning (the use of consequences to modify behavior) to build confidence, teach tricks, and retrain basic obedience skills, which Levi immediately loved and mastered. Along the way, Seward became a better owner and trainer by learning to communicate more effectively with a dog who has aggressive/reactive tendencies. Positive reward-based motivational methods have always been a part of Seward's training, yet Levi has been her biggest challenge. "One big key to my success with Levi was and continues to be anticipation—not ignoring subtle clues that he's giving, and making a point of redirecting him before his issues come out."

Two years after arriving in Fayetteville, Levi is a changed dog—a social butterfly. A narrow threshold for stress still plagues him, yet he handles himself remarkably well at dog shows, which are notoriously crazy, chaotic, noisy environments. And, it turns out Levi loves dog shows! He completed the requirements for his American Kennel Club (AKC) and Australian Shepherd Club of America (ASCA) Companion Dog (CD) titles with all first places. An epic accomplishment because it requires a dog to stand (off leash) for examination by a judge. He also completed his AKC Rally Excellent title, Canine Good Citizen (CGC), and the Australian Shepherd Club of America (ASCA) Rally Advanced X title. And Levi just qualified for the 2015 AKC National Rally Championship.

"The monumental lessons Levi has taught me and his undying willingness to trust me and give one more person a chance to get it right is so rewarding. I love this dog. I am forever grateful for the strange way our paths crossed and for having the courage to follow my gut and bring him into my life. I'm so thankful he found his way home."

He's Never Bitten Anyone!

Is Levi's case extreme? Maybe. Although canine aggression is not as rare as you might think. An estimated 4.5 million Americans are bitten by dogs each year. But why?

You may be surprised to hear that a lot of owners are in denial about their dogs' aggression, with some owners ignoring growls and explaining away snaps and near-misses. "He's never bitten anyone!" is what most veterinarians and trainers hear just before Fido sinks his teeth into a hand. Denial is problematic on many levels, especially for the dog whose future may be a one-way trip to the shelter. Facing the reality of a dog's aggression is difficult for many owners. Some owners are genuinely oblivious to the signs of aggression and the consequences of their dog's behavior. Other owners simply can't fathom that FiFi is aggressive. "Oh, she's not growling. She's just talking! It's really kind of funny." Well, not really, especially if you are on the receiving end of punctured skin. Maybe you have heard similar justifications, such as "He's just playing," or "She doesn't like men." Or maybe you have caught yourself rationalizing a growl or bite? "He was abused as a puppy." Making excuses only puts the dog at greater risk of causing injury.

It's worth clarifying that circumstances may arise when owners want their dogs to show a little hostility, such as telling a stranger to back off or when a shady character approaches them on the street or comes knocking at the front door. Countless stories have been told of dogs who have risked life and limb to save their owners from harm. Assessing the context of the situation, listening to the dog, and trusting his instinct is always a good thing. Lunging, growling, or biting when you pick up his food bowl, tell him to get off the couch, or brush, bathe, or clip his nails is something entirely different.

Did You Know? BITE FACTS

According to the Centers for Disease Control and Prevention (www.ced.gov):

- An estimated 4.5 million Americans are bitten by dogs each year.
- Roughly 850,000 people require medical attention, with half of these being children.
- One in five dog bites results in injuries serious enough to require medical attention.
- More than 27,000 people underwent reconstructive surgery in 2012 as a result of a dog bite.
- Male adults are more likely than female adults to be bitten.
- As the number of dogs in the house increases, so too does the incidence of dog bites.

Aggression Academically Defined . . .

Aggression is defined as a threat or harmful action directed to one or more individuals. Seems simple enough, right? After all, attack-mode aggression is pretty easy to recognize. Few people mistake the significance of a lunging, barking, teeth-baring, snapping, salivating dog. Yet, aggression is a tricky topic because different types of aggression exist. There's defensive aggression, dominance/conflict-related aggression, and possession-related aggression, or what's often called territorial, guarding, or resource-guarding aggression. Protective-type aggression, pain-related aggression, predatory aggression, redirected aggression, and learned aggression are other common forms seen in dogs, as well as in other animals.

Some dogs are dog-to-dog aggressive or display what is sometimes called *interdog aggression*, meaning they are often fine with most people or other animals but fight with other dogs. Intact male dogs frequently posture and challenge each other, and some females simply do not get along with other females.

Further complicating the matter is that some forms of aggression are normal behavior. Predatory drive, for example, is a natural instinct in many breeds, such as terriers. Technically, it is a form of aggression in which breeds have been bred to "go to ground" (hunt and kill vermin). Most people don't have an issue when cats stalk and kill mice or terriers kill rats and gophers. Yet, when a dog's natural predatory aggression has him stalking other dogs, cats, rabbits, or chickens, it's a problem, and there's reasonable cause for concern.

Equally problematic is the not-so-simple act of categorizing aggression because no standardization of diagnosis exists. While people tend to lump dogs into a specific

Some owners do not recognize the signs of aggression in their dog.

category, dogs aren't machines, so it's not quite as simple as labeling a behavior as a particular type of aggression. Because aggression tends to be multifactorial and complex, a dog can exhibit varying signs of aggression at the same time. He may be fearful and angry at the same time, thereby sending conflicting signals.

Is Levi, for instance, truly aggressive, in the sense of being out of control of his emotions, or was he simply frightened? What part do genetics play in his temperament? Absent harsh handling in his younger years, would he still be aggressive? What part chaotic, noisy, fearful shelter environments played in his behavior is equally perplexing.

The Effects of Fear

Most aggression is fear-based, and the fear of being hurt must certainly be one of the most common fears in dogs or any animal. Fearful dogs can be aggressive in the sense of growling and flashing their teeth when they feel

Most aggression is fear based.

threatened. Most often, these dogs, and probably Levi, too, aren't looking to hurt anyone, but rather are simply trying to defend themselves—although, if trapped or pushed too far, many dogs trying to defend themselves will bite if given no other options, such as fleeing. (Think *fight-or-flight* instinct.) It's highly likely that Levi's aggression/fear biting is a behavior learned through harsh and inappropriate handling and training.

Humans aren't always the cause of pain-related fear or aggression. Countless stories have been told of dogs who are otherwise sweet and docile exhibiting aggression as a result of pain related to a sore foot, torn nail, broken tooth, and so forth.

Diagnosing the underlying cause of negative behaviors like shyness, fearfulness, and aggression can be challenging. Pointing the finger of blame at abuse is easy, but it's seldom that simple.

Dogs become anxious, stressed, or fearful for a variety of reasons including a genetic predisposition, lack of socialization, history of abandonment, multiple owners, or any number of anxiety-based disorders. Unfamiliar surroundings, isolation, crowds, strange or loud noises, other dogs and animals, unfamiliar people, and rambunctious toddlers running about can generate stress or fear in an otherwise seemingly docile dog.

Unfamiliar surroundings or people can generate stress or fear in a dog.

It Doesn't Happen Overnight

Granted, some dogs are born with a sour temperament or a skewed view of the world, but, generally speaking, aggression doesn't typically happen overnight. A dog's brain is not hardwired to wake up one morning and think *I plan to bite my owner today.* Or *I think I'll rip my canine sibling's ear off after lunch.* An otherwise normally docile dog doesn't typically "flip out" one day and decide to skin the neighbor's cat.

Signals indicating that trouble is brewing generally start out subtly, such as a curled lip, a low or nearly silent grumble, or an intense stare, but they are overlooked by owners until they increase in intensity and the dog explodes. By then, the damage is done. Many of these dogs are permitted by their owners to develop improper behaviors and subsequently follow a designated path to aggression. For example, dogs do best when they have a clearly defined set of rules and boundaries. Being wishy-washy about the household rules, allowing behaviors at some times and punishing them at other times can create fearful, anxious, conflict-type behavior in many dogs. Dogs are constantly looking to owners for clues on how to act and where to go. If a dog looks to his owner for direction and there is none, he is likely to make up his own rules.

Many experts disagree on the efficacy of formal temperament testing in a shelter environment—mainly because dogs are stressed, anxious, fearful, and so forth. More than a few shelter staff and volunteers lack sufficient training or understanding as to how to implement and/or read the results objectively. Yet, dogs need to be evaluated—which differs from temperament testing—in order to give workers a small glimpse into the dog's personality.

Evaluations, according to dog trainer and shelter expert Robert Cabral, founder of Bound Angels and author of *Desperate Dogs, Determined Measures. Helping Shelters Save More Lives*, can prove more valuable later when formal temperament tests are performed. Yet, in the beginning, shelter workers need to see a basic evaluation. How do they do that? For owner-surrendered dogs like Levi, the shelter may have a tad bit more information, but owners have been known to fudge the paperwork, and many owners are ill-equipped to read or assess canine body language. Cabral offers these suggestions for shelter employees (and you may want to ask whether your potential rescue was evaluated or temperament tested):

- On leash, observe the dog's body language. Does he appear stiff? Relaxed? Withdrawn? What are his eyes doing? Are they darting around the room? How does he look at the environment and the people and other animals around him?

- Offer him a small treat. Does he take it, ignore it, take it and drop it, or become withdrawn or assertive?

- Without speaking to the dog, gently pet his head and upper back. Does he move away? Remain calm, stiffen, or snap at you?

- Make a slight clicking noise with your mouth and observe the dog. Does he engage quickly, withdraw, frighten easily?

- Walk the dog by some strangers (assuming he has no known aggression toward people). Does he look to engage, get scared, or freeze in place?

- Walk him by other dogs (at a fair distance) and watch his basic body language. Does he look to engage in a loose friendly manner? Does he snarl and growl with a stiff posture? Is he indifferent or aloof?

These evaluations provide shelter workers with a baseline reading, so to speak, by giving them some initial readings on a dog and letting them know what they are dealing with. This is especially helpful during a more formal behavior assessment test.

"He's too dominant!" is a frequent complaint heard by trainers, behaviorists, and veterinarians. Dominance is not synonymous with aggression. Most times, the problem is not dominance, but rather opportunity. Dogs learn that certain behaviors, such as curling their lip or refusing to give up a bone have beneficial outcomes: *"This is my bone, and you're not having it."* Each time a dog's behavior has a beneficial outcome, it reinforces his assumption that he is entitled or in charge. He quickly learns that certain behaviors result in favorable outcomes. Often, owners fail to recognize this dynamic is in place. When they intervene, the dog may respond aggressively.

We Never Saw it Coming

Aggression is a serious problem and can escalate from a lip curl to a full-blown attack in the blink of an eye. By learning to recognize the warning signs of impending danger, you can prevent problems by intervening before your dog unloads on another animal or person and, equally important, prevent your dog from being on the receiving end of an attack. Generally speaking, aggression signals can include but are not limited to several or all of these cues:

- Vocalizations (e.g., growling, snarling, barking, etc.)
- Tense, stiff, and/or silent body language
- Tail raised, usually held high over the dog's back
- Ears drawn back
- Lips drawn back exposing teeth
- Strong and direct eye contact

Recognizing less subtle but equally important cues include identifying object guarding (e.g., food, toys, furniture, etc.), which can be as simple as a dog lowering his head or crouching over an object, flicking his eyes, glaring, or turning his head in the direction of another animal. The position of a dog's ears, tail, and hair indicate what he might do, as well as his underlying emotional state, such as fear or anxiety. Pushy, bossy behaviors, such as pawing, nudging, whining, and demanding attention, or ignoring basic obedience commands are indicators that your dog may be headed down a wayward path. Ignoring obedience commands doesn't mean that you have the makings of a serial biter on your hands. However, obeying commands means that your dog accepts and respects you as the leader and is less likely to challenge your authority.

Addressing Common Issues at Home

It seems obvious that using aggression, such as hitting or yelling at a frightened dog, is counterproductive, but, sad to say, people do it all the time. Many owners (and trainers!) subscribe to the popular ideology that the only way to get a dog to listen to you is to make him afraid of you. Not so long ago, hanging a dog by a choke chain or flipping him on his back (i.e., alpha or wolf roll) was an acceptable means of getting him to submit. Some people believe any response other than the one they wanted is an intentional challenge to their authority. Still others feel all dogs crave power, and it is their job to convince a dog he will never have it.

Punishing a dog who is acting out of fear only escalates the fear and makes things worse because, in many situations, it is the underlying fear or anxiety that triggers the aggressive response. A vicious circle ensues for which the dog pays the penalty. The fallout from this type of behavior is that some dogs will stop growling. That's the goal, right? Not necessarily. If your dog is growling, you need to see the world through his eyes and figure out *why* he is growling. (Growling that occurs during a fun game of play is different from growling related to fear, anxiety, etc.) Growling is one method dogs use to communicate fear, to warn us that they are about to blow their tops. Perhaps, for whatever reason, a dog growls because he is fearful of approaching strangers or big white dogs or rambunctious toddlers. When a fearful dog is punished and he stops growling because you have taken away an important component of his communication system, he doesn't think, *"Yikes, that really upset my mom. I better knock it off."* Rather, some dogs become afraid to growl so their body language becomes stiff and silent, until one day they detonate. *"He snapped for no reason!"* or *"There was absolutely no warning whatsoever!"* are common grievances heard by trainers. The growling *was* the warning signal, but he stopped growling because he was punished for doing so.

Is it any wonder aggression is one of the top reasons dogs are surrendered to shelters?

Punishing a dog who is acting out of fear only escalates the fear and makes things worse.

Work with a Trainer or Behaviorist

If your dog is showing indicators of aggression, don't despair. Dogs can change. A carefully designed program of desensitization and counterconditioning can habituate them to the negative stimulus that triggers their fear. Working

with an experienced trainer or behaviorist is essential because of the complexities of aggression. A dog's behavior almost always arises as a result of the complicated interactions between nature and nurture. Owners often run afoul when they attempt to diagnosis the problem themselves. Emotional involvement can cloud owners' judgment, therefore they don't always see the true dynamics of the situation. They may see just one small part of a bigger puzzle. For instance, the problem may be the owner, not the dog. Or, in multiple-dog households, the problem may not be the fearful dog but rather a dog in the background who is triggering the problem.

Working with an experienced trainer or behaviorist is essential because of the complexities of aggression.

Build a Bond

Building a strong human-canine bond will go a long way in helping to build trust, as will instilling basic obedience commands, such as Sit, Down, Come, Stay, in a fun and humane manner. Interactions should be thoughtful, clear, and concise, and dogs should be given the opportunity to signal if they are uncomfortable. Recognizing a dog's low-level stress cues (before they become major stumbling blocks) will tell you when he is uncomfortable, when you can ask a little more, and when you should back off. Always working within a dog's threshold is essential.

Purely positive training is great for puppies or adult dogs who have been trained harshly in the past because it provides a safe way to let them know the rules have changed and that training is fun and, more importantly, safe. Keep in mind that anxiety, fear, and stress can affect the rate at which a dog learns, as well as his performance capabilities.

Simple commands that are reliably performed, such as Sit or Go to Your Bed, can help calm some anxious dogs because it tells them what to do. Food rewards and plenty of

No matter what size, an aggressive dog needs serious help and management.

verbal praise are ideal for rewarding correct behaviors. For some dogs, physical praise in the beginning stages may be too much.

Equally important, pay attention to your own body language. Is your body language angry or fearful? If you are fearful that your dog will eat the mail carrier, your body language will tell him that you are afraid he will eat the mail carrier and cue him to do exactly what you are fearing. Therefore, you should not be shocked or mortified that he ate the mail carrier!

Helping Your Dog to Be Safe

Keeping your reactive or aggressive dog safe is a full-time job. You need to work with an experienced behaviorist or trainer because the consequences are usually too high to go it alone. As a responsible owner, your dog's safety is paramount and includes managing his environment so he is not allowed to get himself into trouble. The more a dog is allowed

If your dog is wearing out his welcome with his unwanted behaviors, consider enlisting the help of a trainer or behaviorist. Most likely, your dog's aggression issues started long before he came to live with you. Helping him to change his behavior so he can be safe and live a happy, calm, confident life is paramount. To help a trainer or behaviorist help your dog, consider these tips:

- Refrain from diagnosing the problem yourself.
- Observe and record (videotaping is ideal) details of what is happening.
- Rather than write "dog is aggressive," record the behavior in detail, such as biting, snapping, ears laid back, tail tucked, etc.
- Record when the behavior happened (e.g., morning, evening, before going to bed, when visitors arrived, etc.) and what you and your dog were doing (e.g., walking, eating, playing, cuddling)

Everything is relative. What you see might mean something entirely different to an experienced trainer or behaviorist.

to fight or practice certain behaviors (growling, snarling, snapping, biting, lunging, etc.), the more practiced and ingrained those behaviors become. Subsequently, the harder it becomes to manage or eliminate the behaviors. An important component of managing his environment includes identifying the trigger (or triggers) that set him off.

Stress and fear are driving factors in aggression, and although you may think a dog's life is pretty cushy, dogs, like humans, can experience stress for similar reasons including:

- Fear of other dogs or animals
- Fear of another dog taking his bone (or toy or his spot on the couch or access to a doorway)
- Dislike of kids, especially noisy, rambunctious ones
- Anxiousness regarding unfamiliar surroundings (e.g., noisy, chaotic environments such as shelters, kennels, dog shows, new households, etc.)
- Fear of or uneasiness in dog parks bustling with chaotic and often aggressive canines of all sizes and temperaments
- Fear of loud noises, including fireworks or thunderstorms
- Fear of unfamiliar people or the constant stimulation of being in a crowd of people
- Boredom (lack of physical or mental stimulation)

Once you identify your dog's trigger (or triggers), manage his environment to eliminate or reduce and minimize those triggers that set him off. Depending on your dog, these stress-reducing strategies may prove helpful:

- Work with an experienced trainer or behaviorist to implement counterconditioning and desensitization (changing your dog's association with the trigger from negative to positive).
- Manage your dog's environment so you minimize his exposure to the stressor/trigger. For example, if your dog is reactive around people or other dogs, avoid venues where your dog is likely to encounter those triggers. If you dog is fearful when visitors arrive, consider confining him in a separate room with a yummy bone or chew toy.
- Avoid dog parks, which are frequently chaotic and stressful for even the calmest dog. If you're at a dog park and your dog begins showing stress or fear, leave immediately. You may feel you have every right to be there, but you accomplish nothing by putting your dog in a position where he can get himself into trouble.
- When in public with your dog, work on keeping your body language calm and neutral. Keep your dog close but avoid tightening or jerking the leash because this will make your dog think that something is amiss.
- Look for ways to engage your dog in fun activities that do not stress him, such as car rides, hiking, jogging, trick training, herding, dock diving, agility, swimming, etc.
- Obedience train your dog. Basic training enables you to better communicate with your dog, which is less stressful for you both.
- Set boundaries and guidelines. Dogs do best when they have guidance and direction because structure and consistency are less stressful to dogs.
- Consider massage, touch therapy, aromatherapy, flower essences, essential oils, or herbal therapy to help calm and relax your dog.
- Consider a Thundershirt or anxiety wrap (similar to swaddling a human infant), which are proving successful in helping dogs overcome fear and anxiety.
- Feed a high-quality food that can help contribute to your dog's behavioral and physical health.
- Build a strong and mutually respectful human-canine relationship.

Chapter 10

Running Away

The name fits. Hollywood is a vision of curly golden sweetness who overcame a scavenger's life in a Los Angeles park, mere steps from the once glamorous movie capital of the world. A mixed-breed with plenty of Soft-Coated Wheaten Terrier and possibly a pinch of Poodle, Holly (for short) now steals the hearts of everyone she meets. However, her life was certainly headed for a traumatic end were it not for the kindness of strangers.

Alone and fearful, Holly's life was all about staying alive by foraging in trash cans. Strangers, many of them homeless themselves, occasionally tossed food to the scruffy dog whose dirty, tangled coat belied her combined aristocratic French lineage and proud Irish heritage. Ironically, early in the Soft-Coated Wheaten Terrier's history, the breed was sometimes referred to as the poor man's Wolfhound because the "poor tenant farmer and fisherman could not legally own any animal worth more than five pounds sterling."

Although it is easy to jump to conclusions about how the young dog ended up living in the rough-and-tumble neighborhood in and around MacArthur Park, the answer remains a mystery. Someone went to the trouble of microchipping (although it wasn't registered) and spaying her, so at one time someone obviously cared for her. Was a gate inadvertently left open? Did she wander away from her home? Did she bolt from a car door or window? Had she been betrayed by humans, dumped or abandoned in a park in the middle of a mega-metropolis—a common practice among badly misinformed owners?

While ignoring the homeless people living in the park, Holly's terrier-crossed-with-poodle instincts knew something was afoot when Eldad and Audrey

HOLLYWOOD (AKA "HOLLY") IS A SOFT-COATED WHEATEN TERRIER MIX.

Hagar, founders of Hope for Paws, a 501 C-3 nonprofit animal rescue organization in Los

Angeles, showed up. Holly hadn't survived all alone on the streets by being foolish. "She wasn't afraid of the homeless people. She knew they weren't going to bug her, but she kept running away from me," says Eldad, who spent hours trying to capture the skittish and terrified stray. Despite Eldad's impressive ninja moves, Holly remained just out of reach. At one point, Holly bolted out of the park and into a busy street. In an attempt to trick the keen terrier mix, Eldad tried blending into the environment by standing next to a homeless man and ignoring Holly. Returning to the park, the edgy girl realized the jig was up a second too late. Eldad lassoed Holy as she darted past him. She quickly chewed through the rope but not before Eldad dropped another slip-leash

HAPPY IN HER FOREVER HOME, HOLLY LOVES OTHER DOGS AND REGULARLY SWIMS WITH HER CANINE BUDDIES.

around her neck. Realizing that if Holly chewed through the second leash, she would be gone for good, Eldad took off running toward his car with Holly in tow. Unable to run and chew at the same time, Holy was safely deposited in the Hagars' car.

Underweight but not emaciated and with no identification, Holly was turned over to the Bill Foundation, also a 501 C-3 nonprofit animal rescue organization in Los Angeles, for fostering and socialization. A much needed warm bath and clipping brought out Holly's naturally stylish good looks. Yet, fearful and terrified of noises, the scruffy stray whose ancestors descended from hardy workaholics nearly jumped out of her skin at every noise. "We had to be extremely careful anytime she was outside on leash because she was so highly reactive, she would hear a noise and bolt, easily slipping out of her collar," explains Lynda Joyce, volunteer and admin coordinator with Bill Foundation. Whether Holly's noise phobia is genetic or learned is unknown, but it's highly likely the "flight" in her genetically inherited flight-or-fight instinct was working overtime as a result of living on the streets.

To flourish, Holly needed a calm environment with an owner who was patient and willing to work with her. Someone who understood positive reinforcement and was willing to give her the time she needed to adjust to her newly domesticated life. Plenty of people inquired, but they weren't the right fit for Holly. After all, rescue is about finding the perfect, forever home.

So how did a street dog from L.A. find the perfect forever home 500 miles (805 km) away in Reno, Nevada?

Sarah Johns wanted another dog, and it had to be a rescue. While in college, she had purchased a Yorkshire Terrier from a breeder, which in retrospect turned out to be a puppy mill dog who was horrible with children. This time, she did her research—researching family-oriented breeds with sound temperaments and hypoallergenic coats. The Soft-Coated Wheaten Terrier fit the bill, so Johns went in search of a rescue. Holly's photo popped up on Petfinder.com, and the rest, as they say, is history. "I loved this dog from the second I saw her picture," says Johns, who immediately filled out the in-depth and lengthy online adoption application. Once approved, Johns, a news anchor for KOLO 8 in Reno, flew to Los Angeles to meet Holly. "It was love at first sight. Within 24 hours, she wouldn't leave my side. She's like my shadow."

Today, the canine vagabond with the once questionable future has crashed high society. The fearful girl has come out of her shell to reveal her true inner superhero. She gets wonderfully silly and fills Johns' life with endless love, and vice versa. She loves other dogs and regularly swims with her canine buddies. (Quite apropos, as the word Poodle comes from the German *pudeln*, meaning to splash about in water; interestingly, the French call the breed *caniche* (from *chien canne*, duck dog), which echoes their early reputation as retrievers.) Holly doesn't mind being groomed and is a complete cuddle bug with a bit of a sassy streak. No doubt a throwback to her terrier heritage!

Of course, even "perfect" rescue dogs come with a few challenges. Holly, who is about two years old, had a few housetraining accidents, which is to be expected, and she barks at people who pass by her fenced backyard. An ongoing challenge, Holly remains a runner, and Johns is keenly aware of the extra security precautions that must be taken to keep her Houdini wannabe safe, including building a strong bond and reliable Come command. Holly remains leery of men, too. She nipped a male neighbor on the ankle and gave another male visitor the stink eye. Johns' dad, who lives nearby, has taken a proactive approach by filling his pockets with tasty tidbits and rewarding Holly any time she approaches on her own terms. Interestingly, she's phenomenal in public, loving everyone, but she remains guarded with men who tread on her turf.

Holly has come a long way since being rescued from her vagabond life in January 2014. She eagerly accompanies Johns on hiking trips in and around Reno's spectacular wilderness areas, and, most importantly, she personifies the perfect pet companion. Positive reinforcement, patience, love, and a boatload of kisses are turning this once skittish stray into a fabulously happy pooch of super intelligence and amazing versatility, synonymous with her mixed bag of Irish, French, and German ancestry.

Managing a High Flight Risk Dog

Ironically, plenty of shelter and rescue dogs are considered runners or high flight risk dogs. Who knows whether they end up in shelters because they lacked a solid recall (Come command) or whether the flight behavior became ingrained in a shelter environment. Depending on your dog's history and, in many instances, his breed, he may be a high flight risk. He may have a history of escaping, which may be how he ended up at a shelter or rescue organization. Many puppies are easily excitable and too young and immature to understand the Come command. They can easily escape and get lost in the blink of an eye. Frightened or startled dogs are high-risk bolters, too. Many dogs are inquisitive, and, once their nose hits the ground, they don't look up until miles later. Some dogs, puppies included, experience longer transition periods and take a long time to get used to a new home, sounds, people, routines, and so forth. Erring on the side of caution and assuming your dog is at high risk of escaping is always wise. Taking precautions—never putting him in a position where he can run off, keeping gates closed at all times, reinforcing fencing, keeping him on leash any time a possibility of escaping is remotely possible, including when you open the front door—will help to keep your bolter safe. Most importantly, begin building a strong human-canine bond and teaching a strong and reliable recall (Come command) right away.

The Recall: A Rudimentary and Essential Skill

A reliable recall allows your dog freedom. Freedom to run and play off leash, swim in the lake, and tussle with his canine buddies because you know he will come when called

Rescue Tip: HIGH FLIGHT RISK

Depending on your new dog's temperament, personality, and past history, he may be a high flight risk. Possibly he has a history of escape, which may be how he ended up at a shelter or rescue organization. Busy, excitable puppies who are too young or lack adequate "recall" or obedience training can easily escape. Dogs who are nervous, fearful, or anxious may try to escape as a means of coping with stress. It can take a long time for some puppies and dogs to get used to a new home, sounds, people, routines, and so forth. If you are uncertain about your dog's history or training, always assume he is high risk for escape and take precautions. Go beyond what you think is necessary, and the odds of keeping your pet off the "lost" list will increase greatly.

A reliable recall is essential.

despite a potpourri of distractions. So important is a strong, reliable recall that it cannot be overemphasized. It literally can save your dog's life.

It's a super-important skill that all dogs must know, regardless of their breed. Sure, some breeds are easier to train and more willing to come when called, but don't think that lets you off the hook. If, for instance, you own a terrier, hound, or husky, you may need to work harder and smarter to develop a reliable recall command. Ok, you will definitely need to work harder and smarter! Call a Sheltie, Australian Shepherd, or Golden Retriever and he is likely to run to you as fast as he can: "I'm coming mummy!" Yet, most terriers, which were originally bred to work independently of their owners, will see no benefit in giving up their freedom and all of the wildly fun and enticing smells associated with it simply to be by your side. The same goes for most hounds, who will find a rabbit more rewarding than any Come command. Siberian Huskies are genetically programmed to run and run and run, kicking up a cloud of dust (or snow!) in their wake, so getting them to come when called is a lofty, but not impossible, goal.

A reliable Come is a simple exercise to teach, yet it's the one behavior that causes many owners a good deal of angst. "Why won't my dog come when I call him?"—it's a complaint trainers hear all of the time. But why? Where owners often run amok is by assuming that a puppy or adult dog comes preprogrammed with a Come command. Sure, it sounds ridiculous, but some owners honestly think their dog should come merely because they say so. Unfortunately, you cannot simply say, "Come" and expect a ten-week-old puppy or a six-year-old untrained dog to come to you. You first need to teach dogs in a fun and humane manner that Come means, "Stop what you are doing and run back to me as fast as you can, right now." Absent sufficient training, dogs have no idea what Come means.

Equally common, owners think saying the command louder and louder will magically solve the problem. When that doesn't work—and it never does—owners resort to chasing their dog while yelling, "Come!" In the dog's mind he thinks "Come" means, "You chase me and I run. Yea! Fun game!" To be successful, your dog must always chase you. Granted, some dogs and owners can chase each other with little or no fallout. Yet, generally speaking, chasing most dogs results in dogs running away from their owners, which is a frustrating and potentially dangerous scenario.

Being successful also starts by discarding any excuses and preconceived notions, including all of your "would of," "should of," "could have," as well as the "ought to" and "because I say so," theories and simply teaching a strong and reliable recall in a fun and humane manner, of course.

Before getting started, consider this point of utmost importance: Come, or whatever word you choose to mean "come to me"— be it "Come," "Here," or "Close"—must always be positive. If you call your dog and he comes, you must always, always praise and reward. If you cannot do that, do not call him. It is that basic. There's no wiggle room, and there are no exceptions. If you call him to you and then correct him, "You are a naughty, naughty boy for chewing my shoes!"—in his mind he is thinking, "The last time I came to her, she grabbed my collar and scolded me. I don't think I'll do that again." Ok, maybe a Golden Retriever or Poodle or Border Collie will come no

If you call your dog and he comes, you must always, always praise and reward.

matter what because their DNA is all about pleasing you. But don't expect most hounds or terriers to come, especially if they smell something fishy like a bath or nail clipping or a dose of foul medication. If your plan includes something your dog is likely to find objectionable, such as getting a bath, taking some medications, or getting in the car to leave the dog park, rather than call him to you, simply go get him.

Be Fun!

At the risk of sounding repetitively redundant (again!), building a strong, reliable Come command means instilling the behavior in an exciting, humane manner so your dog views coming to you as a fun game. Ideally, you want a dog who hears "Come" to think, "Yippee! Yippee! Yippee! Something awesome and wild is about to happen!"

Reinforcing this behavior means being more exciting than anything else in your dog's environment, which is a challenging proposition for some breeds (and owners!). If your dog would rather run off and sniff leaves, you need a super-colossal reinforcement, such as liverwurst, boiled heart, steak, or anything that drives your dog wild. Each and every time your dog comes to you, you need to dole out a dozen or more tiny pieces in rapid succession while simultaneously telling him he's a rock star! For the toy-crazy dog, you will need to engage in a thrilling game of tug as his reward.

The more fun recall games you play with your dog, and the more super-hot reinforcements you provide, the more reliable his recall will be. As with many play-related training games, these fun Come games are rooted in Sylvia Bishop's training philosophy.

Find Me!

The Find Me! game is a modified hide-and-seek game that capitalizes on a dog's natural chase instinct. You can play indoors or outdoors, but when playing outdoors, always play in an enclosed area so that your dog can't escape. Ideally, your dog should be dragging his leash or a long-line, which you can step on should he decide to run off and explore an enticing smell or bug or anything else he finds intriguing. However, sometimes long-lines get tangled around tree stumps or rocks, so you'll need to survey your surroundings and consider the potential risks.

1. Start with a handful of soft, tasty tidbits that are bright enough to be seen when tossed on the ground, such as string cheese, tortellini, or those day-glow cheese balls that come in the plastic barrel.
2. Show your dog the food, then toss it away from you, such as down the hall or across the room or lawn. If they see it, most dogs will run after it.
3. As your dog runs to get the food, run in the opposite direction—go from one room to another or hide behind a chair or a door or, if playing outside, a tree or bush.

The Find Me! Game:
When your puppy or adult dog is distracted—sniffing the grass, eyeing a bird—take off running or duck behind a tree, shed, or whatever is nearby while saying your dog's name enthusiastically. When he finds you, shower him with verbal praise, and a yummy treat or a game of tug.

4. Call your puppy's name enthusiastically, "Fido! Fido! Fido!" Dogs naturally want to chase things that run, and your dog should be stimulated by the excitement of your running away.
5. When he finds you, shower him with praise, "Aren't you clever! You found me!" and a generous smattering of kisses and a jackpot of tasty tidbits or a tug on his favorite toy.
6. Throw another tidbit of food away from you and start the game over.

In the beginning, your hiding spot should be somewhat obvious, making it easy for your dog to succeed. As he becomes more enthusiastic and proficient, make your hiding spots more challenging.

Whereas many dogs, especially herding, hound, and terrier breeds, will chase anyone who runs away from them (which explains why dogs love chasing fleeing children), your rescue may be reluctant to run and find you. In this case, make your voice more inviting and exciting, make it easier for him to find you by letting him see you, or have the person holding your dog run with him to find you.

A modified outdoor version is to wait until your dog is distracted—sniffing the grass, eyeing a bird—and then take off running or duck behind a tree, shed, or whatever is nearby while saying your puppy's name in a happy, enthusiastic tone. When he finds you, shower him with praise and enthusiasm, "What a good Come!" and reward with plenty of yummy treats.

Remember to always progress at a rate that is comfortable for your dog and his individual temperament.

Avoid fussing and trying to fix a mistake in training. It's water under the bridge. Instead, forget about the goof-up and play with your dog to get him in the right frame of mind, then set him up and help him to do it correctly the next time.

Pass the Puppy

This game is a lot of fun for instilling a reliable Come command, especially with young or small-breed puppies, but it does require two people to play.

1. Start with you and a friend sitting on the ground facing each other, with your legs as wide apart as possible and the bottom of your shoes touching. This forms a makeshift chute to guide the puppy. Arm yourselves with tasty tidbits (and a clicker, if you're clicker training).

2. Have your friend hold your puppy (for larger puppies, try holding his buckle collar) as you entice him with a tidbit of food while saying his name enthusiastically: "Yankee, Yankee, Yankee!"

3. When your puppy alerts to you and is looking eagerly toward you and/or straining to get to you, your friend releases him.

4. When he gets to you, pick up his leash, so he can't run off while simultaneously rewarding with verbal praise, "Good Come!" and a tasty tidbit, as well as plenty of hugs and kisses. (If you are clicker training, "click" as soon as your puppy takes his first steps toward you. When he gets to you, praise and reward.)

5. If your dog is not interested in the "game"—tap the ground with your hands, make kissing noises, squeak a toy, or whatever it takes to make yourself more exciting to your dog.

6. Turn your puppy around so he's now facing your friend while you restrain him and have your friend repeat the above steps.

7. Repeat the "game" three or four times in succession. As your puppy progresses, gradually increase the distance between you and your friend, which increases the distance your puppy has to travel to each person. Keep it fun, and it won't be long before your puppy is tearing back and forth across the yard to get to each person.

Playing this fun, interactive game builds enthusiasm, develops your dog's personality and confidence, and builds an intense eagerness and desire to be with you. It helps puppies grow into adult dogs who are willing to climb or crawl over or go through anything to be with their owners.

Chase Recall:

Photo 1—Have someone hold your dog by his leash (do this on a buckle collar, no choke or pinch collars), run to the other side of the yard as you say his name enthusiastically. **Photo 2 & 3**—As you run in the opposite direction, the person holding your dog lets go of him. Encourage him by saying his name in a happy, excited tone of voice. **Photo 4**—When your dog gets to you, reward him with a yummy cookie.

Chase Recalls

Chase recall games are fun, as well as excellent motivators for all dogs. This game, which is a variation of the previously mentioned Fine Me!, utilizes resistance training, as well as a dog's natural chase instinct to instill a fast and enthusiastic recall. Always play this game on a buckle collar—never a choke or prong/pinch collar—to prevent injury.

1. Start by having someone hold your dog's leash. Rev up your dog by showing him a tidbit of food or his favorite toy. Play growl, "Grrrrrr!," and tap him on the chest, and ask him, "Do you want to do recalls?"

2. After you have shown him the food or toy, take off running across the yard as you enthusiastically say his name, "Fido! Fido! Fido!" Most dogs will yip, yap, and lay into their collar because their natural instinct to chase is being incited.

3. When you are about halfway across the yard, turn and face your dog. The person holding your dog lets him go. Continue encouraging him with his name and toy. The goal is for your dog to tear across the yard toward you with a great deal of enthusiasm and excitement.

4. When your dog gets to you, encourage him to run through your legs by tossing the toy or food through your legs. Praise with "Good Come!" Then spin around, grab his toy and play a game of tug for a few seconds, or reward with tasty treats, before repeating the "game" three or four times in succession.

A variation of this game is to follow the above steps, but, rather than turn and stop, continue running away from him as fast as you can (while still keeping an eye on your dog) until he catches you, and say "Good Come!" Or, just before he catches you, stop, bend over, peek through your legs, and say his name. As he runs through your legs, reward him with the food or toy and plenty of praise. Use your imagination to create other fun and exciting variations to the game.

How Often Should You Train?

Frequent but short, fun sessions are best. All you really need are three or four fun recalls multiple times a day to build a strong behavior. For instance, do a few recalls up and down your hallway during a commercial break or while you are outside moving the sprinkler. The key is doing several recalls every day because when puppies or adult dogs are learning new behaviors, it is much easier for them to comprehend and progress through a behavior if you work with them every day. It is important, however, not to overwork them. Always quit while your dog is hyped up and still craving more "fun." This ensures he will be eager to play the next time you call him. If you play until he becomes exhausted or bored and quits on his own, you've played too long.

Adding a Cue

In the beginning, you want to add the Come cue as the dog gets to you. (If you're clicker training, you want to click and reward any forward movement toward you.) This helps to teach the right association. For example, if you are playing the chase recall game and you call your dog to Come, but he decides to veer off and hike his leg on a fence post, you have inadvertently taught him to ignore Come. Instead, in the beginning, give the command as he gets to you: "Good Come!" He will associate coming when called with coming all the way to you. As your training progresses, it should be easy to predict when your dog will come to you straightaway, and then you can begin adding the Come cue

when he's halfway to you, then eventually before the behavior.

If your dog veers off course to sniff some leaves or hike his leg, do whatever you need to do to get his attention back on you. Run away while saying his name, jump up and down, spin in circles, clap your hands, roll on the ground—whatever it takes to get him focused and running toward you. Otherwise, your dog will learn that he can run off and do what he likes whenever he likes without any concern for your desires. (No doubt this is how many dogs end up forever lost!) If your dog is more interested in his environment, decrease the distance he must travel between the people calling

Once your dog is coming when called reliably, start adding distractions like a ball.

him, increase your motivation (e.g., use tastier tidbits or a better toy), and make yourself more exciting by being silly and inviting.

Equally important, your recall cue should sound the same each time. Ideally, a high-pitched, happy Come command will be more inviting than a low, grumbling or militant "Come!" That said, we all know dogs have superior hearing, so it's not necessary to scream at the top of your lungs. Make your voice exciting, but it need not sound like a sonic boom.

Distractions

Once your dog has mastered coming when called in a nondistractive environment, such as your living room or familiar back yard, begin incorporating mild distractions, such as a toy lying nearby or a friend standing nearby. As your dog learns to work with mild distractions, begin increasing the distractions including a cat on the fence. Distractions vary from dog to dog, so you will want to understand your dog's quirks and idiosyncrasies. Some dogs are super-social, and it's hard to resist any friend of theirs who might suddenly appear. A ball lying on the floor may be a minor distraction—say, a two on a scale of one to ten—for an English Cocker, but an eight for a toy-crazy Belgian

For puppies or small breeds that are shy or a bit uncertain about chasing or playing, have the person holding your dog slip his or her hands under the puppy's tummy, holding him a few inches off the ground and encouraging and motivating him by asking him, "Where's your mummy?" As you are running across the yard or room calling him enthusiastically—"Sparky! Sparky! Sparky!"—the person holding him lets him go. As he is running toward you, get on the ground with your arms and legs wide open ready to embrace him with a potpourri of hugs and kisses and yummy treats. By getting on the ground, you become more inviting and less intimidating to him. If necessary, tap the ground with your hands or make kissing sounds to egg on and motivate him. For small dogs, encourage them to climb all over you.

The more you play this game and the more exciting you make it for your puppy, the more confident (and obsessive!) he will be about coming to you. The Come command will not be stressful because you have made it a fun and exciting game.

Tervuren. Some Border Collies are obsessive-compulsive and go berserk at the sight of a fly or a bird. A cat scurrying across the yard might be an off-the-chart-distraction for a terrier, but not a problem for the mellow Newfoundland. A swimming pool, lake, puddle, or even a sprinkler may not bother a Chihuahua but might be a major distraction for a water-loving retriever.

If your dog has a difficult time focusing, perhaps the increase in distractions was too severe. Try playing in a less distractive environment. Or, possibly, you need to make yourself more exciting than the distraction. The long-term goal is 100 percent reliability off leash because one day calling your dog to Come may save his life.

Keep in mind that doing a recall in your backyard is not the same as a recall at a dog park or while hiking in the woods or running on the beach. Owners often go awry by allowing their dogs to go off-leash too soon in distracting or unfamiliar environments. No doubt you have seen dogs off leash at dog parks or beaches. However, unless you are 100 percent certain your dog will come amid chaotic distractions, he should never, ever be off leash. The risk of him running off and becoming injured or lost is too high.

So, before you take your off leash gig on the road—you need hundreds, if not thousands, of super-successful recalls amid distractions, such as dog class, a fenced yard with squirrels scurrying around, birds flying overhead, and other dogs playing and chasing balls nearby. Until then, keep him safe by keeping him on leash or a long-line.

Chapter 11

High Drive, Energetic Dogs

Kota—"Type A" Personality

"Oh Lord, stuck in Lodi again." John Fogerty struck it rich with his 1969 song about a drifter "seekin' fame and fortune, lookin' for a pot of gold" in California's central valley, and so too did Kota, a four-month-old Border Collie picked up wandering the streets of the small agricultural town. Kota's fame and fortune was Tiffanie Moyano, founder of The Shelter Dog Project, a rescue organization in San Jose, California, who bailed out the puppy and granted her a life of gold. Ten minutes before closing time, Moyano tucked the wiggling baby dog under her arm, sealing the puppy's fate. Kota had a home, this time forever. Like the song's fictional drifter, Moyano and Kota set out on the road—not in search of fame and fortune, yet it found them anyway in the form of teammates and agility superstars.

As with many strays, Kota's story is simultaneously familiar and mystifying. An unknown pedigree. No identification. How or why she ended up lost and alone is impossible to say, but someone was missing a fabulous puppy. Surely, her owners would come looking for the mostly black puppy who possibly wandered away while immersed in a potpourri of enticing smells and puppy-dog curiosity. One week passed. Two weeks passed. Three weeks passed, and still no one came to claim the puppy. More than 2,000 animals are brought into the Lodi Animal Shelter each year. An overwhelming, chaotic experience for pets and owners, Kota undoubtedly could have become another statistic had Moyano not stumbled upon her. Too easily, the canny puppy whose ancestors descended from the pastoral borderland between England and Scotland could have ended up with owners devoid of any understanding of the breed's unparalleled intelligence, endless drive and energy, and quirky

KOTA HAS ALL THE TYPICAL BORDER COLLIE TRAITS, INCLUDING ENERGY AND CONFIDENCE.

behaviors, including a penchant for attacking moving objects, be they lawnmowers, weed-whackers, or vacuums.

While Kota is squashing preconceived notions about rescue dogs, Border Collies are not a breed for everyone. Bred for hundreds of years with one goal in mind—improved herding ability—few, if any, ever detox from their state of constant motion. With triple-A type personalities and get-it-done-right-now attitudes, no self-respecting Border Collie stops to smell the roses.

Moyano, an experienced dog trainer, readily admits she lucked out and hit the trifecta with Kota. A quintessential high-drive, high-energy, jumpy, bouncy, happy puppy who knew nothing, yet her attitude spoke of confidence and ability. Embodying the breed's true spirit and character without the insane drive some Border Collies possess, the smart, energetic, jazzy Kota is easy on the eye and full of confidence. Her saving grace is an "off switch" that allows her to settle down after working—something many Border Collies and high-drive, high-energy dogs lack—and a primary reason many of them end up in shelters and rescue organizations.

KOTA HAS TURNED OUT TO BE AN EXCELLENT AGILITY DOG.

Recognizing the breed's heritage as premier sheepdog with unmatched intelligence, stamina, and endurance, Moyano maximized Kota's future by straightaway channeling the puppy's energy into basic obedience, games, play, and agility training. "She's extremely social with a rock solid temperament and is amazing to train," says Moyano. "She's bird crazy, so I joke she's part bird dog, but 100 percent good dog! She is very forgiving and cuts me a lot of slack in training." Moyano's biggest challenge is getting Kota to work away from her—a necessity when competing in many of the advanced agility classes. Three years after being plucked from an overcrowded shelter, Kota and Moyano have developed an unbreakable bond on and off the agility course, earning their U.S. Dog Agility Association (USDAA) starter, advanced, and master level titles capped off by qualifying for the 2014 Cynosport® World Games.

In addition to monopolizing trophies, Kota is the official "unofficial" therapy dog for Moyano's writing class. As owner of a tutoring center, Kota regularly accompanies Moyano to work where she hangs out, providing confidence and gifts of comfort and healing to nervous and anxious students who readily admit Kota is the reason they refuse to miss class.

As with many rescues, the universe seems to have its own formula for them, and life for a wayward Border Collie pup did not include being stuck in a Lodi shelter. Given a full dose of personal attention, good management, direction, guidance, training, and love, Kota stole Moyano's heart and ran with it all the way to the winner's circle. "How lucky am I?" says Moyano. "I hit the jackpot when I found her." The time spent training Kota is unquestionably worth more than gold.

Herding dogs have a strong working ancestry.

Living With High-Drive Dogs

Have you ever noticed that some of the most popular dogs around town (and in the shelters) are dogs with naturally a lot of energy? High-energy dogs are super-popular because talented trainers make owning one look like a walk in the park. After all, who can resist the antics of Fly, the adorable Border Collie in *Babe?* Or the silly shenanigans of *101 Dalmatians*? Unfortunately, living with a Jack Russell Terrier is nothing like living with *Frasier's* Eddie. But it's not impossible. Time, energy, love, patience, direction, and a basic understanding of a breed's origin are all it takes to live harmoniously with a turbo-charged dog. You don't even need Dr. Dolittle on speed dial, but a wildly creative imagination helps because you will need plenty of fun games to physically and mentally challenge and stimulate these blast-mode dogs.

Sure, you're thinking, "What difference does it make what my dog was bred to do? He's not a working dog. He's our family pet." Here's why: Everything about the human-canine relationship comes down to the relationship you have with your dog. Are you wondering why your newly rescued terrier digs in your garden? Or why your energetic Australian Cattle Dog chases and nips the ankles of fleeing children or why he has an obsessive desire to move back and forth behind you? What about that Siberian Husky? Can't figure out why taking him off leash is a nightmare? Wondering why your retriever won't stay out of the water—any water? Are you tired of trying to tire out your shepherd mix?

The majority of today's retrievers, hounds, terriers, and herding dogs—those breeds that typically fall into the high-energy category and now live as family pets—descended from a strong working ancestry. Many of today's breeds retain levels of the inherent characteristics and drive for which they were originally bred, and therein lies the problem: Most of today's dogs no longer have full-time jobs. Most sheepdogs, retrievers, and terriers live in cities and suburbs rather than on farms and ranches, but their innate drive and instinct to work remains. Taking these dogs off the farm or out of a hunting environment does not squelch their desire to work. An energetic, driven dog is energetic and driven whether he lives in the country, city, or suburbs.

**Knowing something about a dog's breed origins
can help channel his natural instincts.**

Dogs lacking appropriate mental and physical stimulation will come up with all sorts
of creative and destructive ways to vent their excess energy, and chances are you will
not like any of them. Chewing, digging, barking, escaping, fighting, and a whole host of
obsessive-compulsive behaviors are counterproductive to living in harmony.

What's His Game?

Understanding your dog's history and origin and the purpose for which he was originally
bred allows you to channel his natural instincts into productive behaviors while
simultaneously discouraging unwanted ones. But what if your rescue is a combination
of breeds? Or, as is the case with many rescues, you know nothing of his ancestry?
That's okay. Basic laws of genetics control the inheritance of most, if not all, canine
characteristics. The traits a dog inherits such as herding, guarding, or retrieving, or even
aggression, dominance, independence, tractability, speed, and so forth depend on the

Wally, a rescue dog from Texas, sure looks like an Aussie mix—but his DNA profile came back and he's actually a Pomeranian-Tibetan Mastiff mix…Honest!

trait's mode of inheritance. Figure out what makes your dog tick by getting in the habit of really watching and observing him at every opportunity. Watch when he is sleeping, sitting, standing, playing with other dogs or children, and eating. Some dogs dislike physical praise. Does yours? Maybe he likes his tummy rubbed and his nose kissed but dislikes his ears being touched. Is he bold? Timid? Does he charge into a room full of energy, bravery, and self-confidence? Is he pushy? Bossy, aggressive, sassy? What's his peak energy time? How does he react in hot and cold weather? What about unfamiliar surroundings and rambunctious kids? Is he inquisitive or curious? Does he hold a grudge? Does he wag his tail and spring to life when he sees you? Hopefully so! Is he a couch potato? Does his demeanor scream, "Must I wag my tail today?" Does he have a great desire to please you, to be with you? Or could he care less about you and your pocket full of treats?

Understanding the soul and essence of your dog will help you to come up with fun and creative games that instill fun tricks and basic obedience behaviors. If, for example you understand a Border Collie's intense herding instinct and propensity to chase moving objects, you can cultivate training games that maximize his chase instinct. If you appreciate that your terrier was bred to go to ground, you can come up with fun digging games to satisfy his instinct to hunt. Knowing your Siberian Husky was bred to run and run and run means you know never to put him in a position off leash where he can run away.

By watching and observing your dog, you may be able to zero in on a few of his innate instincts, or at least his likes and dislikes, and use them to come up with fun games. If you're stumped, you may see any of the following traits in your purebred or mixed-breed dog.

Herding Breeds

Herding breeds were originally bred to control the movement of other animals, primarily sheep and cattle. An abundance of energy means they are usually ready for any activity at the drop of a hat. The sight of a tug toy or ball can send them over the top with excitement. Many herding breeds are *sight sensitive*, meaning that they are acutely aware of movement. Therefore, they tend to like games that involve moving, such as chase recalls and fetching. Many of them literally go nuts when a toy is dragged or wiggled on the ground, and more than a few dogs love tugging.

Terriers

Terriers are feisty, energetic dogs whose ancestors were bred to hunt and kill vermin, with many using their strong neck muscles to quickly shake and kill their prey. Generally speaking, you cannot force a terrier to do anything he does not want to do, so capitalizing on his natural instincts is an ideal way to channel his energy. Most terriers love to play, especially shake-and-kill type games, as well as decapitating or toy shredding-type games. Any type of scurrying movement, like that of a rodent or a toy being dragged on the floor, can make them manic. Channeling his natural instincts and energy can be as easy as teaching him to hunt and dig in a sandbox or a mound of dirt to "find the mousey." Hiding treats or toys around the house or under a box and teaching him to use his excellent eyesight and natural hunting instincts to find them will captivate your terrier.

Did You Know? WHY PLAY IS SO IMPORTANT

Play is essential for the physical, mental, and social development of healthy puppies. Overall, play will help a puppy or adult dog develop into a well-behaved and treasured family member, welcome wherever he goes. Important for improving your dog's overall physical and mental health, exercise and play burn calories, stimulate circulation, build strong bones and muscles, and maintain flexible joints, keeping a dog fit and trim. Exercise strengthens a dog's respiratory system, aids in digestion, and helps get oxygen to tissues. It nourishes and energizes a dog's mind, keeping it active, healthy, and alert. Plenty of exercise and appropriate games between dog and owner can help eliminate loneliness, stress, and boredom, which are primary causes of unwanted behaviors including barking, digging, chewing, and ransacking garbage cans. The best part about play is it's free!

Boxers are a working breed, and are known for their high energy.

Sporting Breeds

Sporting dogs—pointers, retrievers, spaniels, setters—either point, find, or flush game (or all three) on land or water, which means they love retrieving games. The sight of a bumper (a training toy), tug toy, or flying disc can whip them into a frenzy. Pointers "scent" game birds, so try some fun scenting and/or tracking, "find it," or "hide-and-seek"-type games with a fake duck or bird scented cloth, which will encourage his enthusiasm for the game. A sporting dog's training is built on prey drive, so encourage games that instill or increase a strong prey drive such as fetching and chase recalls. Teach him to retrieve the newspaper, your car keys or shoes, or even his dog bowl when he's finished eating. Use your imagination to come up with fun games that encourage holding, such as holding and carrying his favorite toy or even his leash.

Working Breeds

Working dogs, for the most part, were bred to perform jobs such as guarding property, pulling sleds, or performing water rescues. Some pretty high-drive, high-energy dogs are included in this group, including Boxers, Doberman Pinschers, and Rottweilers, to name a few. Encourage games that utilize their natural instincts. Portuguese Water Dogs, for example, were used to drive fish into nets, retrieve lost tackle and broken nets, and act as a courier from ship to ship and ship to shore. The breed's innate retrieving skills and athletic, agile body make it a natural for water games such as swimming or retrieving. Most dogs in this group enjoy "find it" and "hide-and-seek" type games, as well as chase recalls or any games that involve movement.

Hounds

Hounds typically don't pop into mind when discussing high-drive, high-energy dogs. Yet, plenty of breeds in this group can hold their own when it comes to speed, endurance, and agility. Broadly speaking, two types of hounds exist—the *coursing hounds*, such as the Borzoi, Greyhound, Scottish Deerhound, Irish Wolfhound, and Whippet; and the *tracking hounds*, which include the Basset Hound, Beagle, Black and Tan Coonhound, Bloodhound, Dachshund, and less common Harrier, and Otterhound, to name a few. Both originated as hunters of nonfeathered game (deer, elk, bear, foxes, badgers, and hares), but the coursing breeds find their game by sight, "running as silently as death, using all their breath in driving their marvelous legs," while the tracking hounds have keener scenting powers and, generally speaking, are not as speedy; these hounds were usually followed on horseback or foot.

You're not likely to outrun the Greyhound and while most Russian Wolfhounds will live and die without ever seeing a wolf, most coursing breeds still love a good chase. Use your imagination to encourage games that instill or increase a strong prey drive, such as chasing a toy on a long rope, fetching, hide-and-seek, and chase recalls. Some tracking hounds, such as the English Foxhound and American Foxhound, have good stamina and can move at a good clip, so play fun chase recall games, or hide scented cloths and teach your dog to "track" and find it. The less popular Otterhound—"looking like a Bloodhound in sheep's clothing"—chased otters along Britain's fishing streams. Webbed feet lend this breed surging power as he swims, so consider fun water/retrieving games if you own this magnificent breed.

This group's breeds are varied in size and shape. Learn the purpose for which your hound (or hound mix) was originally bred and then use your imagination to come up with fun games that stimulate his natural instinct.

Toys

Originally developed as companions (pets of kings and commoners), toy breeds, many of which are only slightly larger than a bookend, have always been in great demand. Twenty-one breeds currently make up the AKC's Toy Group, and although "toy" is synonymous with small, these pint-sized packages have retained certain characteristics of the larger breeds from which they descended. From the Chihuahua to the Poodle to the Toy Fox Terrier, many of these breeds possess "big dog"

Chihuahuas are part of the Toy Group, but have a "big dog" attitude.

The French Bulldog is one of the more popular members of the Non-sporting Group.

characteristics and can hold their own in terms of speed, endurance, and agility: consider that a diminutive Papillon is the highest ranking agility dog in America!

Highly intelligent and inquisitive, toy dogs need appropriate physical and mental stimulation. For example, Toy Poodles are said to have been trained to dance to music. (It's rumored one Poodle did card tricks back in the day.) What could be more fun than teaching your Toy Poodle trick training or canine freestyle (a popular choreographed performance set to music that illustrates the human-canine relationship)? English Toy Spaniels once showed true spaniel heritage with their skill at hunting woodcock. Your Spaniel may still enjoy hunting, retrieving, chase recalls, or hide-and-seek games. More than a few enjoy obedience and agility.

Toy dogs are portable, so to speak, and playing fun tricks and games that challenge them mentally, such as hide-and-seek, scent discrimination, and retrieving, will help build a strong human-canine bond. Who knows? A canine sporting event may be in your future!

Non-Sporting

Non-sporting is a bit of a misnomer because, years ago, dogs were either of a "sporting nature" or they were not, and those that were not were relegated to the "non-sporting" group. Through the years, the AKC further classified these breeds into the Hound, Terrier, and Toy Groups, and today twenty dogs currently make up the AKC Non-Sporting Group. A diverse group, it is said this group of dogs "must distinguish itself by being so versatile and of such superior quality that it can hold its own to all comers." These dogs are sturdy animals with varying personalities and come from many lands—from China, Tibet, Europe, and America. Some stem from regal ancestors, and others come from humbler caste. Yet, like all non-sporting dogs, this group's principal aim is to please their masters. These true companions include the Bichon Frise, Chow Chow, Dalmatian, French Bulldog, and Keeshond, to name a few.

Don't let "non-sporting" fool you. The Poodle was once a hard-working "water dogge," and your Poodle (or Poodle mix) may still enjoy water games, such as swimming, dock diving, or retrieving, or even card tricks, parlor games, and dancing! The Dalmatian, once a coach dog who challenged highwaymen and cleared the way for this master's carriage, still has plenty of energy and may enjoy chase recall and prey-drive games. Bulldog courage and determination are not idle phrases. Teach your Bulldog fun retrieving or tugging games or—for the truly ambitious owner—give Tillman, the famous skateboarding/surfing Bulldog, a run for his money. Centuries ago, Keeshond's were used to guard barges and catch rats. Today's Keeshond still needs a job, so consider teaching yours to carry the newspaper or mail, fetch your shoes, or "hunt" fake rats in a sandbox to stimulate his mind.

Truly a diverse group, most of the companion dogs in this group enjoy "find it" and "hide-and-seek" type games, as well as chase recalls.

Attention

One of the first "games" you will want to teach your dog is that paying attention to you is fun. After all, without your dog's attention, you cannot teach him anything. Think how annoying it is when you are discussing an important matter with someone who is off in a mentally different land texting or keeping one eye on the television. Dogs are no different, and it is one of the most important reasons you should start right away making yourself your dog's primary motivator of fun.

Show your dog why paying attention to you is advantageous.

Some trainers pooh-pooh the idea, but without your dog's attention, he is likely to wander off and find his own fun. This causes owners a good deal of angst, and it's one of the prime reasons owners give up on training. They claim, "He doesn't listen to anything I say!" or "He's impossible to train!"—neither of which is true.

Attention is a learned behavior, and teaching it is like teaching any other command, be it Sit, Down, Stay, Come, or the like. The not-so-good news is that it can be a lot of work depending on your dog and his temperament and personality. Getting and maintaining attention from a Bulldog, Bull Terrier, or Basset Hound, for example, can take a lot more time and energy than working with a Golden Retriever, Poodle, or Border Collie. The good news is that once your dog is crazy about being with you, focusing on and working for you, your relationship will flourish and teaching him just about anything will become a snap!

You are not going to teach an attention cue or command. Instead, the goal is to keep your dog's attention on you, which means you must be more exciting and stimulating than his surroundings—and there is a lot of competition out there. Focusing on you (i.e., paying attention) is going to become your dog's default behavior. Everywhere you go and everything you do, your dog should be conditioned to look to you for direction and guidance, as well as fun. As your dog becomes more proficient, you gradually begin asking for longer periods of continuous attention. Doing so requires him to learn to ignore distractions, which is challenging for some dogs.

Show your dog a hundred reasons why paying attention to you is advantageous, and he will quickly learn, "Any second my mom is going to throw my ball or spit a cookie or take off running, so I better pay attention!" Making yourself fun and exciting and your dog's primary motivator is an important component of successful dog training.

Try speaking in a high-pitched voice to get his attention.

Working on Attention

In the beginning, when first working on attention, choose a place where there are few or no distractions, such as your yard or living room. As your dog progresses, distractions should be relatively minor, such as placing a toy on the floor or having a friend or family member nearby. Gradually increase the distractions to maybe another dog or person in the room, then eventually the dog or person walking past you, then working in a formal dog class or on your sidewalk or in your front yard. The more you reinforce your dog's attention in a fun, positive manner, the faster he will learn. Eventually, he will focus on you despite other dogs and people, noises, smells, and, yes, even squirrels scurrying up trees.

Most dogs, although certainly not all, like movement. While talking to your dog in a happy voice, hop to the left, hop to the right, step back, spin in a circle, hop on one leg, roll on the ground. Other times, stand still and whisper, "Who's my rock star?" See how softly you can talk while keeping his attention. The quieter your voice, the more intently he has to listen. Other times, talk in a high-pitched voice. "Are you my superstar?" Your dog won't understand the words, but he will respond to your tone of voice.

If he looks away, quack like a duck or bark like a dog. Do a crazy dance! Turn your back on your dog, so he has to run around to see your face. Ask him, "Where were you?" or "There's my silly boy!" If he doesn't run around to see your face, bend over and peek between your legs and say, "I see you!" Show him a toy and encourage him to "get it" as you interact in a quick game of tug.

Encourage him to watch you by being unpredictable. Have a toy stashed on your body, as well as around the yard or house. When he least expects it, quickly pull out a toy. "What have I got?" Have a fun game of tug, or hold him by the collar as you toss the toy, then release him as you tell him to "get it." Run with him to help build confidence. To encourage him to run back to you, take off running in the opposite direction or get on the ground and clap your hands, "Bring it here! Yea! Good boy!"

For very distracted dogs, kneel down and pick inquisitively at the grass or dirt. "Aaaahh, what is that?" Ninety percent of the time, a dog's natural curiosity will get the better of him. When he comes over to investigate, as if to say, "What are you doing, mummy?" kiss his nose and tell him, "I love you!" or touch his toes or toss some grass in the air. Resist the urge to grab or restrain your dog, which could cause him to shy away; in the future, he'll think twice about coming to you.

Spontaneity and enthusiasm will keep your dog's interest and focus on you. Your rescued dog's temperament, personality, breed, and history will dictate your exuberance and level of interactive play. Dogs who are nervous or timid may be reluctant to play. In these instances, try working on getting him to relax and be comfortable around you and the toys. Sit on the ground and let him approach you. When he does, tell him he is brave and reward him with a yummy treat. Working within your dog's limitation is important. Paying attention to you should be fun—not scary!

Fun Games

Play any games that your dog enjoys, as long as they are interactive. Sitting at your table drinking coffee or talking on the phone while your dog chases bugs in the yard is not interactive. Channel the play into learning specific commands or desired behaviors in a fun, stress-free environment. Sure, it takes a lot of energy, but the results are well worth the expenditure.

This owner is illustrating the "What's this?" game.

What's This?

Developed by Sylvia Bishop, one of England's top dog trainers, this game helps to teach your dog to focus on you.

1. Place a yummy treat in your mouth.
2. Put your index fingers to your lips and ask him, "What's this?"
3. When he looks at you, praise him with "Yes!" (or click if you are using a clicker), and reward with the treat from your mouth.

Spitting the treat at your dog is great fun, too, especially if he is proficient at catching. You can then begin incorporating "What's this?" into your Come command. As your dog is running toward you, put your fingers to your lips and ask, "What's this?" Make the game fun, and it won't be long before your dog is racing to get his treat.

Twist and Spin

With both the twist and spin, the dog spins in a circle on command, as if chasing his tail.

Teaching a dog to twist is a simple, fun command that helps to increase his vocabulary, stimulate his mind, and pay attention.

1. Start with a tasty tidbit of food in either hand, between your thumb and index finger. With your dog standing, hold the treat close to his nose and simply guide him in a counterclockwise circle, keeping his head low.
2. When he completes the circle, tell him "Good Twist" (or click) and reward him with the tasty tidbit.

It's that simple. The goal is to get him twisting on command without luring him with the food, which is accomplished through repetition and consistency. Once he can do that without any luring, gradually begin increasing the distance between you so that you can give the command Twist from first 1 foot (30 cm) away, then 2 feet (60 cm), 5 feet (152 cm), and eventually from across the room. Spin is the same game but rather than moving counterclockwise, the dog moves—or spins—clockwise.

Once he has mastered the Spin and Twist, try incorporating a Sit. For instance, have him spin then sit, or twist and sit.

Key Point: You (and your dog) may find it easier if you hold the treat in your left hand when twisting counterclockwise and your right hand when spinning (clockwise). This way your dog can move forward into the turn and be on the correct side of your body coming out of the turn. Plus, you can impress your friends when you signal your dog with one hand and then the other.

Training Tip: TWIST AND SPIN TROUBLESHOOTING

If you have problems getting your dog to twist or spin, consider breaking the behavior into smaller steps.

1. With the cookie in your left hand (for the twist) or right hand (for the spin), encourage him to move either clockwise or counterclockwise by moving the treat level with his nose backward as far as his shoulder.
2. Once he's moved that far, praise (or click) and reward.
3. Now lure his head farther toward his tail until he takes a step with his front feet. As he steps, praise (or click) and reward.
4. This time, ask for more of a turn by luring his nose past his tail position so that he has to step around with his front and hind legs.
5. As soon as he passes the halfway mark, praise (or click) and reward.
6. Once he passes the halfway mark, he's likely to continue the circle on his own so that he comes around to face you and receive his treat.

Food on the Floor

When you have a high-drive dog, you can never have too much focus. Here's another fun game to help you show your dog how much fun watching you can be.

1. Start with your dog on a short but loose leash (short enough so that his head can't reach the ground but not so short that you are restraining him). For small-breed dogs, kneeling on the ground so you are at his level works well.

2. Feed your dog two or three yummy treats in a row, and then drop one on the floor. *Cookie. Cookie. Cookie. Oops, dropped one!*

3. Don't be surprised if your dog dives for the ground trying to snatch up the treat. Because your leash is short, he won't be able to reach it. He will stare at the treat for a few seconds to a few minutes (depending on his tenaciousness), as if willing the treat to jump in his mouth. Wait him out. Bite your tongue, if need be, but don't say a word.

4. When he looks back at you, say, "Good boy!" or "Yes! (or click if you are clicker training) and reward him with a treat from your hand.

5. Repeat this "game" four or five times. When you are done, pick up the treats on the ground and feed them to him. Do not let your dog eat the treats off the ground because this defeats the purpose of the exercise.

Back Up (Walk Back)

Teaching the Back Up is fun, and, once mastered, it's quite impressive and a highly underrated behavior. Anytime you want your dog out of the way, ask him to back up. Does he crowd the door or gate as you're trying to come or go? No problem. Ask him to back up. Is he a bit pushy, always squeezing past you? Ask him to back up. Depending on your dog, teaching this game on leash so you can maintain control may be necessary.

1. Hold a tasty tidbit between the thumb and index finger of both hands, holding the food about knee high. Bend your knees to make a small chute.

2. With your dog standing and facing you, let him sniff or nibble the food. As he does, take a small step toward him, causing him to move backward.

3. As he takes a step backward, praise with "Good Back Up!" (or whatever command you choose to use) and reward with the food.

4. Repeat several times, eventually getting your dog to step back a few steps, then a few more, and eventually a few more until he can take a dozen steps backward.

Play this game a few times each day, always stopping before your dog becomes bored or frustrated.

As he becomes more proficient, the goal is for you to stand still and have him back up upon hearing the cue without you taking a step toward him. When he does so, toss the treat behind him and tell him to "get it." This reinforces him moving backward.

Once your dog has mastered the back-up behavior, begin adding additional cues. For example, ask him to back up, then sit, or back up then down, or back up and then twist or spin. Or, for the really adventurous, ask him to back up and then wave. Use your imagination to incorporate fun behaviors into the back-up command that stimulate his brain.

Depending on your dog's personality and your commitment to playing the game, it can take a few days to a few weeks, or longer.

Shaping the Back Up

Many trainers are proponents of *shaping* rather than luring. You're teaching the same back-up behavior but rather than speeding along the process by luring (i.e., stepping into your dog), you are shaping the behavior by catching the dog in the act and clicking and rewarding. In other words, watch for your dog to take a step backward. As he is in the act of stepping backward, click and reward. Don't be surprised if your dog barks at you just before or while he is stepping backward. Shaping can be a frustrating task for many dogs, and barking can be an outlet for that frustration. Your dog may also decide to back up and sit, which is okay, if that's the behavior you want. Clicker training/shaping requires spot-on timing because the behavior you click is the behavior you reward, which may not be the behavior you want. If you want only the back-up behavior, you will need to be quick with the click.

Go with the Flow

Owners often run into trouble when they get a breed that doesn't suit their personality and then attempt to turn the dog into something he is not and never will be. For example, attempting to eradicate a herding dog's passion for herding or a terrier's quest to dig is fruitless. On the other hand, trying to establish behaviors that are not endemic to a particular breed, such as expecting a Bulldog to guard sheep (or even move quickly!) or a Saint Bernard to possess the upbeat temperament of a Bichon Frise, is equally fruitless. As corny as it sounds, learning to love your dog for who he is with all his quirks and idiosyncrasies will go a long way toward building a mutually trusting and loving human-canine bond and a harmonious living environment. Learn to recognize his habits, peculiarities, likes, and dislikes and maximize them to your advantage. Life will be much, much easier and enjoyable.

Chapter 12
Special Needs

Thirteen years after being abandoned in a Bend, Oregon, motel room, Maty, a three-legged Australian Shepherd mix, is still giving back to the community that helped to save her. In addition to being a supreme athlete, Maty has become a canine ambassador for amputees. Drawing people in with her own disability, Maty is helping to break down the barriers associated with pet and human disabilities.

Maty, like countless other disabled dogs, could easily have become yet another discarded dog languishing in an animal shelter—another statistic. Having survived tremendous adversities including exposure to the canine parvovirus, a staph infection, and amputation of her hind leg—all before eight weeks of age—life seemed to have its own plan for Maty. Amazed by her courage and perseverance, owners Lynne Ouchida, Community Outreach Manager for the Humane Society of Central Oregon, Bend, Oregon, and Troy Kerstetter, Director of Operations at the Foothills Animal Shelter in Golden, Colorado, adopted Maty in 2001 and quickly found out how much of a survivor this puppy would be.

For a short period of time before being adopted by Ouchida and Kerstetter, Maty was the hospice puppy at a local nursing home, where she provided comfort every day to those in need—the mentally ill, the emotionally distraught, the sick, the disabled, the elderly, and the lonely. Like a true therapy dog, she helped people to smile, to laugh, and to reminisce

MATY HAD TO HAVE HER HIND LEG AMPUTATED WHEN SHE WAS JUST A PUPPY.

about their own animals. Without dipping too deeply into the anthropomorphic well, Maty seemed to sense emotions in humans on a level that is unusual, and comforting those in need seemed a priority. She even refused to leave a person's room for the last few days of his or her life. Some people will say Maty provided gifts of healing and comfort and understood her role as guardian and shepherd of the dying. Others will see it as yet another example of crazy dog lovers being hopelessly and foolishly and, almost certainly, romantically anthropomorphic. Either way, Maty knew intuitively what to do and how to bring comfort.

Interestingly, experts recognize the connection between oxytocin, the "feel good" neurohormone, and the chemistry or emotional state of love. Produced in the hypothalamus, a person's level of oxytocin increases when dogs or other animals are present, and petting a dog can double some people's levels of the feel-good hormone— making them feel warm and overwhelmed with loving feelings. It stands to reason that dogs like Maty can sense their innate ability to calm people.

IN 2006, MATY BECAME THE FIRST DISABLED DOG TO QUALIFY AND COMPETE IN THE HYPERFLITE-SKYHOUNDZ WORLD CANINE DISC CHAMPIONSHIP.

While Ouchida and Kerstetter never set out to make their dog a canine ambassador, Maty proved once again that life had a plan for her. As the Humane Society of Central Oregon's goodwill ambassador, she connects with people by visiting local schools and events and educating the public about the humane treatment of pets. Maty's special gift is touching people, especially kids, with her heart and soul and demonstrating that people and animals with disabilities are just like everyone else. Possibly a throwback to her early months as a hospice puppy, Maty loves being petted, so normally fearful or hesitant kids are able to touch her stump and ask questions. They quickly lose their anxiety and confusion regarding amputees. They realize Maty isn't different, and having only three legs doesn't slow her down. As with the nursing home patients, Maty, instinctively or otherwise, is drawn to differently-abled kids in need. Perhaps she senses the commonality that ties them together.

Making their three-legged dog a Frisbee dog was never Ouchida and Kerstetter's intention. However, once again, Maty's purpose in life seemed to follow its own path, marking her a messenger of passion and self-belief. Her natural athletic ability and her love of jumping and retrieving catapulted her into the national spotlight. In 2006, she became the first disabled dog to qualify and compete in the Hyperflite-Skyhoundz World Canine Disc Championship. Making phenomenal athletic leaps with only one hind leg, she placed seventh out of a class of twenty-five of the world's top canine athletes. In a repeat 2008 performance, she finished in a three-way tie for seventh in a field of thirty elite four-legged competitors. She was so good, many spectators didn't even notice she was missing a leg!

Sushma, a nine-year-old girl from India who had been adopted and brought to the United States, watched from the sidelines. Like Maty, Sushma was an amputee—missing a leg and both her hands. Adapting to change was difficult and challenging for Sushma. People pointing, staring, and making cruel jokes triggered further withdrawal for the young girl. Life changed when she met Maty, who immediately started working her magic on the disabled girl. Tossing Frisbees for Maty to catch, Sushma was laughing and smiling for the first time in a long, long while.

"Maty tries hard at everything she does even though she only has three legs," Sushma later wrote to Ouchida. "Although we're missing a few body parts, we shouldn't be looked down on because we're just as special."

Who would have thought that a puppy abandoned in a motel room would overcome life-threatening misfortunes to teach and provide gifts of healing to disabled people and pets? At thirteen years old, Maty is slowing down, but she continues to show the community that saved her that the roughest of roads are filled with beautiful gifts. "I believe Maty survived all of her adversities so she could bridge the gap and demonstrate the abilities of disabled people and animals," says Ouchida.

If oxytocin helps to explain why some people and dogs seem to be more loving than others, is it possible that Maty has an unlimited supply—or at least a double dose—coursing through her veins?

Living with a Disabled Pet

If your disabled dog lived in the wild, his chance of surviving would be pretty grim. The survival of the fittest philosophy would not serve him well. Thankfully, today, many disabled pets live a relatively normal, happy life. Dogs who are born with a disability, or acquire it early in life—like Maty—don't know they are different. They simply adapt and negotiate life as busy, happy, normal, fun-loving dogs. At least, that's what we assume. The theory is that dogs quickly adapt physically and mentally because in their world no social stigma exists with disabilities, and most dogs are motivated to continue a relatively active lifestyle. Plenty of clear evidence is emerging that dogs experience a wide range of emotions, and no one knows for certain if dogs know others dogs are disabled or different. Even then, it is highly unlikely that they care.

Dogs can have the same types of disabilities as humans, with the more common being blindness, deafness, or loss of one or more limbs.

Loss of Limbs

Seeing a three-legged dog tugs at our hearts, but many of these dogs appear perfectly happy and quite adept at doing everything their four-legged counterparts do. Some even do more—like Hooker, a working Australian Shepherd who, at five years old, lost her right front leg due to osteosarcoma (bone cancer). Within one month, she was back working (on three legs) and placed second in the nation in intermediate sheep and started duck competitions. There's also Dallas, a one-year-old Chihuahua, turned into the San Jose Animal Shelter with a broken front leg and rescued by Tiffanie Moyano. The leg was amputated at the shoulder but that doesn't slow down this feisty boy who hikes four miles (6.4 km) a day, runs with his two Border Collie siblings, and is training for future agility competitions.

Dogs can lose a limb for any number of reasons including human cruelty or an accident, such as getting hit by a car or falling from a balcony. Untreated fractures can become septic, requiring amputation. Many cancers, including osteosarcoma, require limb amputation. Some puppies are born with a neurological disorder or congenital disability or occasionally are inadvertently injured shortly after birth by their canine mothers.

Although many dogs negotiate life quite well with a missing limb, amazing feats of engineering and adaptive technologies can now restore a dog's four-leg mobility. Just like Colonel Steve Austin, *The Six-Million Dollar Man:* We can rebuild him. We have the technology! Ok, so your dog won't have Austin's speed or bionic limbs equivalent to the power of a bulldozer, but engineering and veterinary science are revolutionizing prosthetics for pets.

The use of prostheses and orthoses in veterinary medicine is not a new concept, but, until recently, the majority of fabricated devices were made by human rehabilitation

If you're looking to rescue a pet, don't overlook disabled ones, be they amputees or sight or hearing impaired. These dogs may require a little (or a lot) of extra patience and attention, depending on their disability, so go into it with your eyes wide open. As with their normal-bodied counterparts, disabled pets are beautiful souls who have plenty of love to share, and they, too, are looking for a permanent, loving home. Depending on their disability, they may not be able to jump for a Frisbee or run agility, but they can provide plenty of the healthful benefits dogs provide including:

- **Companionship**: Caring for a dog, or any animal, provides comfort and often takes the focus away from your own problems, especially if you live alone. Disabled dogs can touch the lives of the lonely and provide the same silliness, love, kisses, and cuddles as any dog. They're great listeners, too, which is good because plenty of people talk to their pets (even if they don't admit it). And, of course, nothing beats a wagging tail and dog kisses!

- **Exercise**: Disabled dogs, or at least most of them, usually love walking, too. Studies indicate that taking a dog for a walk is a fun way to fit healthy daily exercise into your schedule, and dog owners are more likely to meet their daily exercise requirements than are non-dog owners.

- **Reduced anxiety**: Canine companionship can provide comfort, help to reduce anxiety, and build confidence—especially for people who are anxious about venturing into public. A disabled dog may help you to overcome your own disabilities.

- **Added structure**: Dogs need regular care and that means you need to take care of them—regardless of how your day is going. You may be stressed, anxious, tired, sick, or whatever, but your dog is counting on you to feed, love, and care for him.

- **Stress release**: Remember oxytocin, the "feel-good" neurohormone produced in the hypothalamus? Studies show a person's level of oxytocin increases when dogs or other animals are present, and petting a dog can double some people's levels of this hormone—making them feel warm and overwhelmed with loving feelings.

Chances are, when you adopt a disabled pet, you may learn a few things about unconditional love along the way.

Disabled dog using specially designed cart for mobility.

professionals. Technology has advanced in the past ten to fifteen years to produce a substantial veterinary science. For instance, *osseointegration*, a process that fuses a prosthetic limb with an animal's bone, has in the past ten years been pioneered by veterinarians and engineers at North Carolina State University. The permanent implant allows the prosthetic limb to attach without chafing or irritation, giving the limb a more natural range of motion and increasing the likelihood of the dog thinking the prosthetic is an original appendage.

Consider also that the not-too-distant future may bring advances that allow a dog's muscles to control the prosthetic's movement. In other words, a dog could "lock and unlock" the artificial joint using his muscles. As with most scientific advances, cost is always a factor and a $100,000 price tag is likely to be cost prohibitive for most owners.

The Benefits of Prosthetics

A prosthetic isn't just a cool thing: it serves a functional purpose, too. While many dogs adapt well to missing or nonfunctioning limbs, their success depends a lot on which limb (or limbs) and how much is lost. Dogs bear 60 percent of their weight on their shoulders (divided by two legs). Dogs missing a front limb often appear to get along well by learning

Rescued Chihuahua Dallas doesn't let his disability slow him down. Keeping up with his four-legged Border Collie siblings, Dallas trains in agility and will be competing in the not-too-distant future.

to "tripod" with their remaining front leg and hind legs, but your dog may not be doing as great as you think.

Short- and long-term consequences associated with overcompensation include breakdown of remaining limbs, such as wrist (carpus) or hock/ankle (tarsus) instability or collapse; chronic back, neck, and muscle pain; weight gain; and, in some instances, premature death. Super-stoic dogs are masters at concealing their pain, so their aches and agony are likely to go unnoticed by owners. Ninety-five percent of pain associated with overcompensation can be relieved with a prosthetic. By distributing weight equally to both sides of the body with a prosthetic, a dog is better able to exercise and have a healthier life.

In the past, amputation often involved removing the entire limb. However, advances in canine prosthetics have veterinarians rethinking the level of amputation because whether or not a dog is eligible for a prosthetic limb depends on the level of injury and how much bone remains. For front or hind limbs, 40–50 percent of the radius/ulna or tibia/fibula must be present. Absent sufficient bone, it's not possible to provide a prosthetic limb. In these instances, dogs may benefit from adaptive devices, such as a light-weight wheelchair that is well suited for hind leg problems, neurological issues, and larger dogs, or a rolling harness that utilizes wheels to provide mobility in dogs with missing or nonfunctional front limbs.

Rehabilitation

Like humans, dogs adapt pretty well to a prosthetic limb, with some dogs figuring it out right away, while others take more time. Success rates improve greatly when dogs work with a certified veterinary rehabilitation person, which requires a minimum six-month owner commitment. Rehabilitation includes dogs learning to recognize the ground through the prosthetic; stepping up and over and clearing obstacles; sitting, lying down, and standing up; maneuvering stairs, getting in and out of vehicles safely; and managing different surfaces, such as grass, gravel, sand, carpet, hardwood, and more.

What You Can Do

Plenty of options exist for you to help your canine amputee. For starters, what dog doesn't love a good massage? Gently rubbing your dog all over, even if you don't know what you're doing, may help to relax his entire body. To go beyond stroking and massaging, consider learning some Tellington-Touch (TTouch) techniques. It's not necessary to understand anatomy to be successful, and it's quite easy to learn. No doubt your dog will love it, too! A popular touch therapy developed by Linda Tellington-Jones, TTouch is based on circular movements of the fingers and hands all over the body. It's designed to "activate the function of the cells and awaken cellular intelligence—a little like 'turning on the electrical lights of the body,'" according to www.ttouch.com.

You may decide to go one step further, as did Hooker's owner, Katie Van de Sandt, who was so motivated to help her dog after she lost her leg to cancer, she enrolled in massage therapy school and became a certified small-animal massage practitioner and now runs her own business.

Plenty of herbal and essential oils are also available such as, rosemary, dandelion, horsetail, and plantain, which may help to reduce inflammation, as well as aid in bone and joint issues.

Don't overlook less traditional yet popular forms of rehabilitation including acupuncture, energy therapy, or Reiki, which require an experienced practitioner.

Making Your Home Safe

Depending on your dog's breed, his size/weight, and which limb (or limbs) was amputated, you may need to make a few adjustments to make his life and yours safe and functional.

- Add non-skid/non-slip rugs to slippery floors, such as hardwood, tile, or vinyl— especially stairs and traffic areas your dog uses to get to his food bowls, dog bed, and for going outside and coming indoors.
- Add baby gates to restrict your dog's access to stairs while you're not around to supervise.
- Consider specially designed stairs or ramps that allow your dog easy on/off access to couches and beds, as well as getting in/out of your car.
- Depending on your dog's size, consider a specially designed harness that allows you to help your dog get up from a down position.

Blindness

Canine blindness can result from trauma, eye infection, cataracts, or an underlying medical condition such as diabetes. Some eye diseases, such as progressive retinal atrophy (PRA), an inherited retinal degeneration, and glaucoma are two common causes of permanent blindness. Collie eye anomaly (CEA), another inherited disorder, is common in smooth- and rough-coated collies, as well as in other breeds, and it may or may not affect a dog's vision. Many cases of blindness are thought to be genetic or breed-specific. The merle gene that is responsible for the beautiful coat and eye colors in some breeds including the Australian Shepherd, Shetland Sheepdog, Great Dane, Catahoula Leopard, Dachshund, and others, is also responsible for many developmental eye defects.

As with humans, a dog's loss of vision can be sudden or progress over time, and be unilateral (one eye) or bilateral (both eyes). With acute vision loss, bilateral loss of vision is more common, but unilateral vision loss can occur, particularly when the other eye is blind. Frequently, owners will report sudden-onset blindness, although an ophthalmic examination may reveal changes associated with chronic, long-standing disease.

You may think blindness is a handicap for dogs, but it need not be. Dogs have senses that are much more sensitive than ours. They can hear and smell way better than humans, and these highly refined senses can help them adjust to loss of vision. In fact, some experts say a dog's blindness is harder on his owners than it is on the dog because

Rescued Border Collie Sparkle lived a happy, well-rounded life despite losing her eyesight at three years of age because of medical issues.

eyesight is actually number three in terms of importance behind a dog's hearing and sense of smell. For humans, loss of vision appears to be more of a hardship because ultimately some independence is lost, such as the ability to drive. But dogs are already dependent on us to drive them everywhere!

How well a dog responds to blindness is influenced by multiple factors including the pattern of blindness (i.e., gradual or sudden), the dog's age and general health at the onset of blindness, previous training, and the age, health, and personalities of other animals in the house. Dogs who lose vision gradually appear to adjust better than those who lose vision rapidly. Such was the case with Sparkle, a three-year-old rescue Border Collie who, at three years of age, went blind as a result of medical issues. Yet she had no problem keeping track of her owner's whereabouts on a ten-acre farm.

Certainly there are activities a blind dog will be unable to do, such as jumping up and catching a Frisbee, but he can still tug it. With patience and proper training, blind or partially blind dogs can still fetch toys, navigate stairs, jump on and off the bed, find their food and water bowls, climb in and out of the car, go for on-leash walks, and tussle

Blind in one eye, Australian Shepherd Chetter is a force to be reckoned with on any agility course.

with their canine buddies. Consider, for example, Chetter, an Australian Shepherd who is blind in one eye due to a merle-to-merle breeding. Yet this one-eyed speed demon is a force to be reckoned with on any agility course.

Blind dogs have a few special needs, including a protected environment. They aren't fragile, so forget the bubble-wrap. However, vigilance in supervising them is paramount, because swimming pools, ponds, balconies, and traffic are serious hazards. One tool that may give you peace of mind is a small alarm that attaches to a dog's collar to alert you if he falls in a swimming pool. Keeping your dog on leash (or harness) when outside will go a long way toward keeping him safe.

Unfortunately, Steve Austin's bionic eyes are not an option in veterinary medicine (yet!). Prognosis for dogs with vision loss is highly variable and depends a good deal on the underlying cause of the condition. For instance, dogs who are born blind (congenital blindness) will remain blind.

What You Can Do

Plenty of options are available that will help your blind dog adjust to his new situation.

- Announce your presence when entering a room or before touching him by talking or saying his name. Walking with a heavy foot to make vibrations may help to alert him that you are approaching.
- A small bell or two attached to you and other family members and pets will alert him to everyone's whereabouts.
- A large floor mat for your dog's food and water bowls may help him to identify their location.
- While on a short leash, walk him around the house to help him "map out" his surroundings. Be sure to offer plenty of treats for being successful.

Nuclear sclerosis: A common disorder of a dog's lens. You might have noticed a hazy gray or blue appearance when you look at your aging dog's pupils. Often confused with cataracts, nuclear sclerosis does not impair a dog's vision to a recognizable extent.

Sudden Acute Retinal Degeneration Syndrome (SARDS): A lesser known cause of sudden blindness in dogs, SARDS is most often diagnosed in older dogs. The median age for the condition is 8.5 years of age. The cells of the rods and cones of the retina suddenly undergo programmed cell death or apoptosis, yet the etiology is unknown and poorly understood. Inflammatory, autoimmune, or allergic causes are suspected, but have not been confirmed. Miniature Schnauzers and Dachshunds are particularly susceptible.

Homozygous Merle Eye Defect: Merle ocular dysgenesis is a group of eye defects found in homozygous merles—dogs who carry two merle genes as a result of breeding a male merle to a female merle. Mathematically, the odds are that one out of every four puppies produced from a merle-to-merle breeding will have either an eye or hearing problem. These defects occur in varying degrees and combination and include microphthalmia (abnormally small eyes), retinal dysplasia (an abnormal development of the retina, resulting in its folding and detachment), abnormal shape and position of the pupils, irregularities of the iris, cataracts, incomplete development of the optic nerve and blood vessels supplying the eye, and lack of a tapetum (the part of the eye that helps dogs to see at night or in dim lighting.) These defects are often associated with or accompanied by excess white markings on the puppy's head, especially around the ears and eyes.

- Check your house's indoor and outdoor layout to eliminate any hazards that could injure him, including sharp edges on furniture, electrical cords, low hanging branches, and the like.
- Use non-slip strips on slippery stairs both indoors and outdoors.
- Carpets or throw rugs can alert your dog to doorways, stairways, and other obstacles, and serve as demarcation lines to keep him from slipping.
- Leaving the television or radio on while you're away may provide him with some comfort and security.

- To avoid confusing your dog, settle on a furniture arrangement and stick to it!
- Teach him new tricks using a ball or toy that contains a squeaker or other noise maker. Try placing a scent on his toys so he can easily find them.
- A bandana or vest that says, "I'm blind" will alert others of your dog's condition.
- In addition to his regular collar, an "I'm blind" tag on his collar will alert anyone who finds him should he become lost.
- Take every opportunity to educate the public, such as asking people to let your dog smell their hands before they pet him.
- Most importantly, be patient. Love him and help him by creating a sight-impaired-friendly and stress-free environment.

Deafness

Deafness is another common disability, and, as in people, canine deafness can be unilateral or bilateral, acquired or congenital, gradual or sudden onset, and transient or permanent.

Congenital deafness (present at birth) is frequently linked to an inherited defective gene that is associated with coat color/pigmentation patterns. An estimated eighty dog breeds are affected with congenital deafness, with some breeds being more susceptible than others. Potentially, it can appear in any breed but especially in those dogs with

Did You Know? BREED PREDISPOSITIONS FOR DEAFNESS

Your dog's white or merle coat color is frequently a factor in congenital deafness, with two pigmentation genes linked with canine deafness:

- The *merle gene* seen in the Australian Shepherd, Collie, Shetland Sheepdog, Dappled Dachshund, Harlequin Great Dane, American Foxhound, Old English Sheepdog, Norwegian Dunkerhound, and others

- The *piebald gene* seen in the Bull Terrier, Samoyed, Greyhound, Great Pyrenees, Sealyham Terrier, Beagle, Bulldog, Dalmatian, English Setter

- Not all breeds with these genes are affected. The deafness usually develops in the first few weeks after birth while the ear canal is still closed. Deafness usually results from degeneration of part of the blood supply to the cochlea, where the cochlea nerve cells die and cause permanent deafness.

white or merle coats. Such is the case with Mooch, an all-white Boxer/American Bulldog mix who was born deaf. Picked up as a stray at nine months old, Mooch lived in a kennel at an animal shelter until he was bailed out by a West Coast Boxer Rescue. During the next nine months, he would be adopted and returned to rescue four times, with each owner confessing a deaf dog was simply too much to deal with. Two owners never gave him a chance—returning him within twenty-four hours of adoption. To help increase his odds of finding a permanent home, Mooch was sent to Dawn Rennie, founder of Enzo's Acres, a Portland, Oregon-based nonprofit rescue organization, for training. Rennie fell in love with him and officially adopted him in February 2014. Straightaway, she went to work building a mutually trusting human-canine relationship and instilling basic obedience commands via hand signals. Today, at two years old, Mooch accompanies Rennie to work daily and helps to bring a calm balance to aggressive or highly reactive dogs. "He is such a great dog," says Rennie, "I get two or three inquiries a week from people wanting to adopt him, but he's not going anywhere."

American Bulldog-Boxer mix, Mooch was born deaf and went through four owners before finding his forever home with Dawn Rennie, Enzo's Acres.

Also falling under the umbrella of acquired congenital deafness are puppies who go deaf as a result of intrauterine infections, drug toxicity (ototoxicity), liver disorders, or other toxic exposures before or soon after birth.

Dogs can also lose their hearing as a result of trauma to the ear components, noise-induced trauma (such as fireworks or explosions, etc.), tumors, infections to the middle or inner ear, or some aminoglycoside antibiotics frequently used to treat life-threatening infections. Less common causes of acquired deafness include general anesthesia or diseases such as canine distemper. Deafness also may occur as a result of excessive amounts of wax, dirt, hair, or other material plugging the ear canal, ear mites, and old age.

Symptoms, Diagnosis, and Treatment

Surprisingly, deafness can be tricky for some dog owners to assess because many of the symptoms mimic the behaviors of untrained dogs, such as not coming when called, not paying attention, and so forth. Frustrated owners often dismiss these behaviors as being willfully naughty or disobedient.

Young puppies often follow their littermates everywhere, so, frequently, owners don't realize a problem exists until they begin obedience training. A few of the more classic telltale signs include a dog not responding to noise, such as the clanging of bowls, jangling of keys, or clapping of hands. Like Mooch, many dogs who are born deaf (as opposed to losing their hearing later in life) do not understand the body language of other dogs, such as barking or posturing. As a result, some dogs play aggressively or bite too hard because they aren't deterred by the other dog's yelping. Some deaf puppies may not wake up at nursing times unless they feel vibrations or are bumped by a canine sibling.

If you suspect your puppy or adult dog has hearing issues, consult your veterinarian. He or she may be able to perform a Brainstem Auditory Evoked Response (BAER) test that detects electrical activity in the cochlea and auditory pathways in the brain, much like an antenna detects radio or television signals or an EKG detects electrical activity of the heart.

For a list of facilities that offer BAER testing, visit www.lsu.edu/deafness/baersite.htm.

Currently, no treatment is available for permanent deafness. The use of conventional hearing aids and cochlear implants in dogs has been anecdotally mentioned, but they have not been met with great success. The devices cost $20,000–25,000, which, even if it the procedure were practical, is cost-prohibitive for most owners. Regular ear cleanings to prevent the accumulation of dirt, wax, or hair in the ear will help to prevent controllable causes of deafness.

What You Can Do

For dogs young or old, be patient and work on teaching nonverbal cues, such as hand signals that correspond with the Sit, Down, and Come commands. "Deaf dogs are not difficult to train," says Rennie, Mooch's owner. "Developing a relationship is the most important thing you can do. Most deaf dogs, especially deaf rescues, need to learn to trust again." Interestingly, like "normal" dogs who choose not to respond to a stranger's verbal commands, some dogs, including Mooch, will not respond to a stranger's hand signals, only to those given by his owner. So don't be surprised if your deaf dog chooses to ignore the commands of people he doesn't know!

Deaf dogs startle easily, too, so flicking room lights on and off can help to get their attention when they're fixated on a cat, staring out a window, chewing a bone, and so forth. Sleeping in a crate provides comfort and security. To wake Mooch, Rennie gently blows in his face so he slowly and calmly awakens to her scent.

Vigilance in supervising your deaf dog is essential. While he may be safe from dangers indoors, he is more likely to suffer injury outdoors because he cannot hear you calling him, or the sound of traffic, beeping horns, and other warning signs. Keep him safe while in public by having him on leash at all times. Always err on the side of caution by steering clear of public dog parks, which can be dangerous and overwhelming for deaf dogs.

Resources

Books

The AKC's World of the Pure-bred Dog. New York: Howell Book House, 1983.

Cabral, Robert, *Desperate Dogs, Determined Measures*. Bound Angels, 2012.

Kaminski, Patricia and Richard Katz. *Flower Essence Repertory*. Nevada City, CA: The Flower Essence Society, Earth-Spirit, Inc., 1994.

McConnell, Patricia B. *For The Love of a Dog*. New York: Ballantine Books, 2007.

Mery, Fernand. *The Life History and Magic of the Dog*. New York: Grosset & Dunlap, 1968.

The National Geographic Book of Dogs. Washington, DC: National Geographic Society, 1958.

The New Complete Dog Book (American Kennel Club). 21st edition. Irvine, CA: I-5 Press, 2014.

Scanlan, Nancy. *Complementary Medicine for Veterinary Technicians and Nurses*. Ames, Iowa; Blackwell Publishing, Ltd., 2011.

Scott, John Paul and John L. Fuller. *Genetics and the Social Behavior of Dogs*. Chicago: The University of Chicago Press, 1963.

Scientific Journals/Papers

Beck, Alan M. "The Ecology of Stray Dogs: A Study of Free-Ranging Urban Animals," York Press, Baltimore, 1973 [re-published by Purdue University Press, West Lafayette, IN, 2002].

Elanco-Lily Market Research, February 2006.

Gaultier, E. *et al*. Comparison of the Efficacy of a Synthetic Dog-Appeasing Pheromone with Clomipramine for the Treatment of Separation-Related Disorders in Dogs. *Veterinary Record*, 2005.

Heath, G.G. "Canine Limb Prosthetics and Orthotics—Design and Outcome." *Proceedings of the European Society of Veterinary Orthopaedics and Traumatology*, Munich, Germany, 2008.

Horwitz, Debra DVM, DACVB. "Canine Aggression and Assessing Dog Behavior: Using What You Already Know to Help Clients." St. Louis, Missouri.

Nash, Holly, BVSc. "Acupuncture in Small Animal Practice." 2011.

Overall, Karen, MA, VMD, PhD, DACVB, CAAB. "Storm Phobias." *DVM 360*. September 1, 2004.

Schwartz, S. "Use of Herbal Remedies to Control Pet Behavior." International Veterinary Information Service, 2000.

Tremayne, Jessica. "Prosthetics Advance with Osseointegration." *Veterinary Practice News*, June 17, 2014.

Verner, Beth and Emily Holden. "The Soft-Coated Wheaten Terrier in America." *ShowSight Magazine*, March 2013.

Young-Mee, Kim *et al.* "Efficacy of Dog Appeasing Pheromone (DAP) for Ameliorating Separation-Related Behavioral Signs in Hospitalized Dogs." *Canadian Veterinary Journal*, April 2010.

Websites

The American Kennel Club Canine Health Foundation
www.akcchf.org

Centers for Disease Control and Prevention: Dog Bites
www.cdc.gov/homeandrecreationalsafety/dog-bites

Louisiana State University: Articles on Canine Deafness
www.lsu.edu/deafness

The Merck Veterinary Manual
www.merckmanual.com/bet/emergency/ acute vision loss

The Orthopedic Foundation for Animals
www.offa.org

OrthoPets Orthotics and Prosthetics for Animals
www.orthopets.com

Note: Page numbers in **bold** typeface indicate a photograph.

home environment safety, 205
homeopathic remedies, 137–143
homozygous merle eye defect, 209
honeysuckle flower essences, 139
Hooker, Australian Shepherd, 201
Hope for Paws, 162
Hope's story, 76–78, **77**
horses, introducing dogs to, 22–23
hounds, 186–187
housetraining
    accidents, 106–107, **106**
    age for, 102, 105–106, **105**
    breed size and, 107
    Come command after pottying, 105
    crate training, 98–100, **99**
    medical issues, 107
    outside pottying, 104
    paper training, 101–102, **101**
    plan for, 103–104, **104**
    Queso's story, 94–96, **94–96**
    schedule for, 102–103, **102**
    techniques, 97–105
    verbal cues, 105
Humane Society of Central Oregon, 198–199
Hyperflite-Skyhoundz World Canine Disc Championship, 200

I

impatiens flower essences, 139
indoor introductory meetings, 17–19, **18**
interdog aggression, 150
introductions
    to cats, 21, **22**
    to children, 19–21, **20**
    creating safe environment, 13–14
    dedicating time for, 23
    to family members, 19–21
    in-home precautions, 18–19
    to horses, 22–23
    to household pets, 21–22
    J'mee and Jake's story, 10–12, **10–12**
    meeting indoors, 17–19, **18**
    meeting outdoors, 15–18, **15**, **17**
    to other dogs, 14–15
    transition period, 16

J

J'mee and Jake's story, 10–12, **10–12**
Johns, Sarah, 164
Journal of Applied Animal Welfare Science, 97, 100
Joyce, Lynda, 163

K

Kerstetter, Troy, 59–60, 198–200
Koch, Katharina, 95–96
Kota's story, 178–180, **178–180**

L

laser acupuncture, 137
lavender essential oil, 140
Levi's story, 146–148, **146–147**
Lily Bella's story, 26–28, **26–28**
limbs, loss of, 201–205, **203–204**
little-dog syndrome, 36
Lodi Animal Shelter, 178
Lucy II's story, 110–112, **110–112**

M

Matty's story, 198–200, **198–200**
McConnell, Patricia, 36
medical issues, housetraining, 107
medications, for separation anxiety, 131–132, **131**
merle gene, 210
merle ocular dysgenesis, 209
milk thistle herbal remedy, 143
mimulus flower essences, 139
Mooch, Boxer/American Bulldog mix, 211, **211**, 213

Photo Credits

Front Cover: Jessica Drossin Photography (top); Sinseeho/Shutterstock (bottom)

Shutterstock: soyna etchison, 1; Tatiana Katsai, 8; Soloviova Liudmyla, 14; CBCK, 15; Fotokostic, 17; dezi, 18; Sergey Lavrentev, 20; VP Photo Studio, 22; Olga Phoenix, 25; Pshenina_m, 32; Little Moon, 33; Annette Shaff, 34; Pavel Hlystov, 37; WilleeCole Photography, 39; Julia Kuznetsova, 43; pixbull, 46; Joy Brown, 51; Amy Rene, 53; Jaromir Chalabala, 57; BestShots, 64; Susan Schmitz, 67; oblak, 69; wvita, 70; llaszio, 72; Boulder Photo, 75; Gelpi JM, 78; pirita, 80; Erik Lam, 82; Jake Sajko, 84; Eric Isselee, 85, 128, 187, 197, 213; Halfpoint, 86; Nathan clifford, 88; Pavel Hlystov, 89; Daisy Daisy, 93; Jagodka, 99; Anneka, 101; Peter Kirillov, 102; otsphoto, 104; Mila Atkouska, 105; Suzi Nelson, 106; Anna Tyurina, 109; Susan Schmitz, 115; MCarper, 116; Annette Shaff, 123; Jaromir Chalabala, 125; Donna Ellen Coleman, 131; dogboxstudio, 132; Reflective Photos, 133; Tanyastock, 135; Anthony Hall, 136; Marilyn Barbone, 138; Arman Zhenilugev, 141; tjasam, 143; Katoosha, 145; Kristina Stasioliene, 150; hd Connelly, 151; aspen rock, 152; Nejron Photo, 155; Rock and Wasp, 156; mdmmike, 157; tsik, 161; Ross Stevenson, 166; Anetapics, 167; Mat Hayward, 170; Adam Edwards, 174; Mark O'Flaherty, 177; Kamil Macriak, 181; Guenter Albers, 183; otsphoto, 186; Aneta Pics, 188; Susan Schmitz, 189; Africa studio, 190;

Barb Riebold Photography: 208
Chantal Reed: 184
Cloud 9 Photos: 199
Dawn Rennie: 211
Dean Lake Photography: 146, 147
Jerry Boysen: 41, back cover (third from top)
Jessica Drossin Photography: 110, 111, 112
Katharina Koch: 94
Ken and Leah Stafford: 58, 59, 60, back cover (second from top)
Kim M. Kehoe Photography: 40, 42
Kimberly Teichrow Photography: 30
Lynne Ouchida: 198, 200, back cover (bottom)
Robert Grzesek: 124, 125
Sarah Johns: 162, 163, back cover (top)
Tiffanie Moyano: 178, 179, 180, 204
Tracy Libby: 5, 10, 11, 12, 26, 27, 28, 47, 50, 55, 63, 65, 66, 77, 95, 96, 118, 121, 169, 172, 192, 203, 207, 212

Tracy Libby

Tracy Libby is an award-winning writer and photographer whose work has won multiple awards from the Dog Writers Association of America (DWAA) and the Alliance of Purebred Dog Writers (APDW). She holds a Bachelor of Science degree in Journalism from the University of Oregon and has been writing about pet care for more than two decades. Her articles have appeared in mainstream magazines including *Dog Fancy*, *Modern Dog*, *Dog World*, *Puppies USA*, *Dogs USA*, and the *AKC Gazette*, as well as online for Embrace Pet Insurance.

She lives in Oregon with her husband, five cats, and five Australian Shepherds. She has been involved in the sport of dogs for nearly three decades, exhibiting her Aussies in agility, conformation, and obedience.